A Spade is a Spade

The Down To Earth Garden Book

Caroline Currie

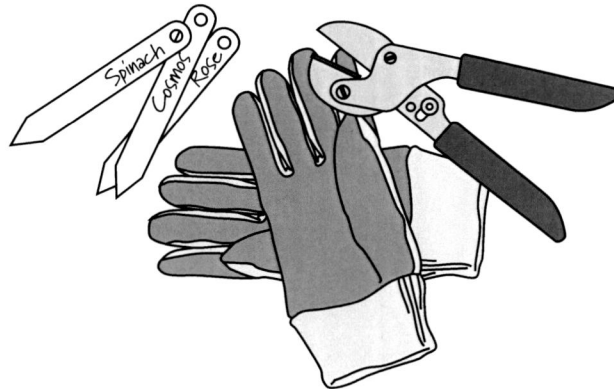

Blue Check Books

Ma, Meryl Currie, in typical position. I learnt it all from her.

Introduction

"Is your garden finished now?" a neighbour regularly asks me at the bus stop. I try not to look at her as if she's landed from another planet. *"Finished"? A garden?*

And one of my friends always says: *"Surely, Caroline, you haven't been out in the garden this afternoon? It's been so windy/wet/cold/hot/…"*

My name is Caroline Currie. I am an ordinary common or gardener from the Planet Earth. I have muddy knees, muddy green gloves, filthy old boots, grubby hat and jacket whose pockets overflow with green string. I am out in my Salisbury garden in most weathers, OK not all, and no, like any other, it is never "finished."

I am nobody famous, I have never passed a gardening exam, or done a course, I hate heathers and hanging baskets, I adore pruning roses, I'm passionate about clematis, my lawn is a disaster, I give a home to families of goldfinches in my plum tree, a mistle thrush in my mistletoe, and gardening is what I love doing most in the world. I think I was born deadheading and I intend to die with secateurs in hand. I have learnt everything I know (and there is lots I don't) by doing it.

A Spade Is A Spade was originally written two years ago at the request of my nephew Hugo, who wanted to know the secrets of the dark arts of gardening, as he put it. Updated and totally revised, it is now an account of the year in my garden from 1st November 2010 to 31st October 2011. Beware, it is highly opinionated, and as the title warns you, candidly written, in plain language. It covers the basics, month by month, what I notice, jobs to do, how to do them, the bad guys, shady characters and the wild bunch, ending with an appendix of my favourite plants. I also have a Mission, capital M: if you are uncertain about your garden, I want to encourage you just to get out there, and just to do it, no matter what the result. We are part of nature and it does us good to live closely with Mother Nature, whatever the bloody weather. I hope you will find joy in your successes, and shrug your shoulders at disasters, mysteries and mistakes, as we all have to. Shit happens. Seize the day.

Acknowledgments

Thanks to Hugo Currie for suggesting this book; Sara Carnegie-Brown, whose comments have helped me produce it; Nicky Howard-Jones for taking the How To photos; Sam Roberts for some of the others; Charlotte Moreton for the back cover pic and assistance in choosing the front; Julie Horne and Sue Newnham of Salisbury Printing. And I wouldn't be a gardener without Ma, Meryl Currie, who first made me get down on my knees in the herbaceous border and taught me to recognise a blackbird's song.

Caroline Currie
Salisbury November 2011

Published by Blue Check Books, Salisbury
www.bluecheckbooks.co.uk
email: info@bluecheckbooks.co.uk

ISBN 978-0-9571124-0-7

Printed by Salisbury Printing, Greencroft Street, Salisbury, Wiltshire SP1 1JF
Tel: 01722 413330

Contents

January

God Almighty first planted a garden, and indeed it is the purest of human pleasures.

Sir Francis Bacon, 1561 – 1626. Of Gardens.

Am I alone in being heartily glad when Christmas and New Year are over and we turn the corner of the year and look forward? I am ready to spot the tiniest glimmer of hope that the days are getting longer, and walk around the sleeping garden searching for snowdrops and swelling buds, and start to think about the changes I'm going to make, and the gaps I'm going to fill where plants have been zapped in the bleak midwinter.

2011

1st   Back to the garden at last, snow gone, ground thawed. Bliss.

2nd   Goldcrest on 'Mermaid' at my window.

4th   Blackcap at my window,
Mrs, brown head. Mr around too,
feasting on mistletoe.

6th   Came in at 4.25 – a little later every day.
Leucojum and snowdrops pushing
through. Blackbird grabbing grape.

9th   Seed potatoes on sale.
Start saving eggboxes for chitting.

13th   Yellow mahonia, red cornus stems,
red-berried cotoneaster on roundabout.
First snowdrop.

18th   Still light at 4.50.

25th   First winter aconite and primrose.

28th   Nuthatch climbing tree and flock
of redwings on Greencroft (park.)
Fat white bud on 'Lulubelle' camellia.

THE WINTER GARDEN I type this through a pair of pink woolly gloves. It is the 4th of January 2011, I have just been out to refill the bird feeders with sunflower hearts, and feel my hands, they're frozen. Has it ever been such a winter? My new Yaktrax crampons and skisticks are in the hall, awaiting the next ice age.

But the garden is miraculously coming to life. Close examination reveals green buds on the lilac, pink pricks on the paeonies, some clematises with buds, and imminent flowering on the white chaenomeles. We need to do this. After a whiteout December with all day hoarfrost, continuous minus temperatures, and frozen effing pipes, it is easy to sink into the slough of despond and the slothful habits acquired through enforced internment. I sympathise with the hedgehogs: hibernation has its attractions. But. But! There is a world out there still left for us. The tits are chattering: if those miniature feathered buggers can survive this shit, so can we.

A NEW GARDEN We all walk into a strange plot from time to time, unless we live in flats, and gaze about us with wild horror or delight. My nephew Hugo and his wife Andrea just have, and are. Where to start? Sissinghurst owner Vita Sackville-West's principles were:

Be ruthless: chuck everything in the second year which didn't do well in the first. (*Come on, Vita, give it a chance: some things take a while to get established.*)

Don't be too tidy: The point of a garden is a fine carelessness. Let plants self seed, or act as 'volunteers' as the Americans call it, yuck, allow some wild flowers. Foxgloves, forget-me-nots, love-in-a-mist and eschscholzia (*try saying that after a glass of Pinot Grigio*) – Californian poppies, in zinging oranges and yellow – will all look after themselves.

Have a plan: start with the shape of the garden, then think about colours and what's out when.

You get back what you put in. True of plants and of people.

All excellent principles. I'd like to add the following **Ten Simple Rules**, which I've evolved over a lifetime of trial and disastrous error:

1. **Get out there.** Nothing replaces just wandering about.

2. **Think about it** for a year when you first move in. Gaze out the window and see what comes up.

3. **Clear the decks**, cut back the undergrowth, you'll be able to see the space you've got a lot better, and maybe make some discoveries.

4. **Keep grass mowed** – like making a bed, it tidies your mind.

5. **Get out there** and think about it some more. Which way does your garden face? Sunrise, east; sunset, west; all day sunny, south; gloomy, north.

6. **Learn to ID weeds**, one at a time, and keep pulling them up, or digging them up (see bindweed in **March**), a little every day.

7. **Preparation is everything.** Don't even think of planting until you have laboriously prepared the ground. Hack, weed, dig. Be patient. The more preparation you do, the better. Concentrate first on area you can best see from indoors.

8. **Make a list of jobs** you feel confident with, and take on one, ie roses or lawn, and do in easy stages of say twenty minutes to half an hour. And bear in mind the wise words of Meryl Currie: finish one job before you start another.

9. **Peer into other people's gardens**, and visit local ones. Be inspired by what grows well in your area, and by books, mags, and tv programmes.

10. **Get out there again.** Do you want to change anything?

What not to do

1. Panic.

2. **Go to garden centres** – yet. Wait and see what comes up, what needs moving, and after a year of discovery and calm thought, make a shopping list; try not to buy on impulse.

3. **Be tempted** by *Telegraph* offers. Buy plants when you can see and handle them.

4. **Be tempted** by seed or bulb catalogues at this stage.

5. **Accumulate pots** – they need too much watering.

6. **Accept everyone's cast-offs** – you could get lumbered. Fine if they've got what you're looking for.

7. **LOOK UP!** Stay out of the A & E eye clinic. Look up to see what you're doing, then shut your eyes. Or wear goggles.

PRUNING APPLES AND PEARS Darkest winter is the time for this, when the trees are dormant. Chop out all interior branches – the same rule for all pruning, to allow light and air to get to the centre. Main branches chop as much as you like off, to get to the right shape (always diagonally, just above an outside bud) and side shoots spur prune, ie to 3 or 4 buds. This encourages fruiting on the short spurs. Loads of things fruit or flower on spurs, eg peaches, and wisteria. Feed after pruning with blood, fish and bone and a bag of manure.

SURGERY FOR LILACS One of my all time old-fashioned favourite trees. I have a big single purple one in the front, and a purple and a white one at the back. All were desperate for the light, tall, pathetic, entangled with sycamore saplings, flowering just at the top. The first year Peter the tree surgeon got rid

My neighbour's mahonia – twelve feet tall.

Winter aconites – out this year on 25th.

First primroses.

3

JOBS THIS MONTH

- Spray winter wash on fruit trees, to prevent winter moth laying eggs. Keep it up once a month till buds about to burst – probably March.

- Prune lilacs and fruit trees while dormant. Follow up with a bag of manure, 6-X, and/or blood, fish and bone.

- We dig dig dig dig dig dig dig, dig, dig the whole day through. If it's fine and ground ain't frozen. Tickle up the beds with a fork to loosen compacted earth.

- Good month to tidy up shed. And scrub tools. Yeah yeah. Well, it's got to be done sometime. Oh, all right then. Please yourselves.

- Scrub out ponds.

- Cut old hellebore leaves off.

- Check ties and stakes.

of the sycamores, and in the second started to saw off one of the main trunks on each to about the height of the trellis (6 ft.) Come the spring, up they sprung, and flowered the following year, on a healthier and much better shaped tree. After this drastic treatment I emptied a bag of manure around the trunk, plus some blood, fish and bone. Other than that, they don't need or like pruning, though you can dead head them if you have nothing better to do, ha ha, after they flower in May.

SCENT IN THE GARDEN And did I mention the scent of the lilacs? How wonderful to bury one's face in the scent of a flower, and I do that a lot at lilac time. If a plant can be both stunning and smelly, that's a real bonus. Roses, lilies, lavender,

eleagnus, daffodils, narcissi, pinks, stephanotis, honeysuckle, philadelphus, wisteria, freesia (don't try growing, hopeless), etc. Go for it if you can. I have never got down on my hands and knees to see if snowdrops have a scent, but my (late, alas) hero Christopher Lloyd of Great Dixter, The God of Gardening, says they smell of honey if you bring a few into a warm place. What that man didn't know.

And seeing as it's January, try mahonia, winter honeysuckle, *Daphne odora* and winter sweet (chimonanthus.) Bring a few branches indoors and give yourself a sensual experience. A bunch of daffs in a jug will give you this, as well as the hope that we're on the turn and winter will eventually end, please God.

FROGLIFE AND PONDS My frogs live in a orange washing-up bowl, with a couple of rocks so they can climb out. I provided this when I realised the garden was overrun with frogs, or are they toads?, in spite of having no water. The smallest amount is gratefully received. Old washing up bowls are also useful for carrying weeds or plants, collecting rainwater, and soaking new plants before planting. I have a collection in gruesome colours.

Pondweed will multiply from a small handful nicked from a neighbour over the summer, and

Frogs in the pond– or are they toads?

Early hellebores, a welcome sight.

Pulmonaria, one of the earliest things out, loved by bees.

help keep the water clear. A bunch of watercress does the same trick, apparently. Or barley straw, obtainable from aquatic garden centres or a harvested field. Frogs vacate the pond in the autumn, so any time from then on is the moment to clear out the dead leaves fermenting on the bottom and give it a good scrub, including the rocks. I have a frog family living under my log pile too, and keep upside down broken pots as sanctuaries throughout the garden.

HELLEBORES Lurking under last year's leaves and all the dead crap at the bottom of the garden you will find fat hellebore buds poking through the wintry earth. Cut all the old leaves off to reveal them. Soon they will reliably spring to life. How welcome they are. Some years they will seed and babies galore will sprout up around them; remove

a few and pot up in order to give them a chance, then replant somewhere. Some, if not most, years they won't, and I am told the seeds germinate faster after a spell in the freezer. They also take a few years to flower. Christopher Lloyd used to cut the stems off, dip the bottoms in boiling water for 30 seconds, and they would flower indoors. Worth a try, as otherwise you have to crawl on your belly to look into their modestly drooping freckly faces.

Thought of the month

Wash hands and remove thorns immediately you get in from the garden. And top up your tetanus injection. It's easy to get infections from cuts and scratches.

February

There is always in February some one day, at least, when one smells the yet distant, but surely coming, summer. Perhaps it is a warm, mossy scent … or it may be in some woodland opening, where the sun has coaxed out the pungent smell of the trailing ground ivy, whose blue flowers will soon appear, but the day always comes, and with it the glad certainty that summer is nearing, and the good things promised will never fail.

Gertrude Jekyll, 1843 – 1932. Wood and Garden

February: some people's most hated month, and sometimes the most bleak and wintry. Don't tell me: you're going on a Noro Virus cruise. Phew, I'm staying put. In February early daffs begin to come out, and suddenly snowdrops carpet the woodland verges. A few more camellias brave the frosty mornings. The dawn breaks a little earlier each day and the sun sets a little later. Winter can be beautiful.

2011

6th Snowdrops on verge of A27 en route Romsey. First camellia out, white 'Lulubelle.'

7th Coots building on Avon. Swans skittish and grooming in the sun.

8th 6.45 am: tiny tweet of dawn solo, still foggy and dark.

11th Blackbird taking centre stage as dawn chorus tunes up. Same date last year.

12th Sheets flapping on the line, everyone in their gardens. Spring?

15th First pink camellia, 'Rose Parade'.

18th Yellow croci carpeting College roundabout.

19th Forsythia in bud. Sara's pond full of fornicating frogs.

20th *Daphne odora* out: its sweet scent drifts across the garden.

24th First mow – of moss. Fuzzy green willows.

25th Bumble in mahonia flowers.

26th Blackcap still with us – grappling with a mistletoe berry.

PRUNING CLEMATISES First of the month, secateurs akimbo, on your marks, get set, go! All the later flowering clematises, ie from July-ish onwards (pruning group 3 in the books), flower on this year's growth, and need to be cut right back to about a foot from the ground, above a pair of buds, so they can start all over again. Drag all the dead stuff down from the fence or the tree (never look up, avoid A & E), stuff it in a bag or barrow, and move on to the next. Ignore the buds and new shoots: they will regrow, springing up from where you cut them. What a great clean-up for spring job this is. And wha-hey for *Clematis viticella*: no wilt, no problems, loads of different ones, chop 'em all back hard this month. I recommend 'Perle d'Azur', pale mauve, which will grow on north facing walls; 'Elvan', tiny purple bell-like flowers, massively scrambling up my apple and out the top; 'Polish Spirit', purple and prolific, covering another old apple and much else in my shady corner bed; and perhaps the most beautiful of all, 'Etoile Violette', velvety deep purple, fantastic with lemon yellow 'Leverkusen' rose. Hard pruning (this is what it will be called on the plant label) encourages them to grow more and more stems from where you cut them and also from the ground. (See **July**.)

The same treatment applies to *C.texensis*, which crawls but doesn't climb, and the even later flowering bright yellow *C.tangutica*. Lovely as the fluffy heads have been, and popular with the goldfinches, now is the time to hack 'em back, and they will return bigger and even better than last year.

Early flowering ones, like *C. alpina and macropetala*, that flower on last year's growth (pruning group 1) are simply tidied up, lightly clipped after they've flowered, or you can do it now. Chop off weak stems and dead growth – if you can tell, most of it looks dead in Feb. Trim the branches down to where you can really see the flowers. The same advice applies to pruning group 2, the big flashy fellas that come out in May and June, which also

flower on the previous year's growth. *Clematis montana* flowers on every branch, old and new. Trim it back after it's flowered, in about May, but if you feel like tidying it up more, fine.

After pruning, feed each with a handful of Sulphate of Potash. Caddick's Clematis Nursery recommend at least a gallon of liquid fertiliser (ie Tomorite) per week in the growing season, but stop when in full bloom. Bloody hell, how can one keep that up? Maybe try once or twice after Sulphate of Potash. Never let them go short of water. When planting, sink a plant pot or a bit of drainpipe a foot away, for water and liquid feed. Give bonemeal and manure in autumn.

Caddick's Clematis Nursery, Lymm Road, Thelwall, Warrington, Cheshire WA4 2TG. Telephone 01925 757196.

Another good one is **Thorncroft Clematis**, The Lings, Reymerston, Norwich, NR9 4QG. Telephone 01953 850 407. www.thorncroftclematis.co.uk. Both do mail order.

PRUNING WISTERIA Twice a year for this mad scrambler: first, in August, cut the side shoots down to about 6 inches long, spur pruning to encourage flowering, and tie in main growths. Now it's time for the second go: cut them back further to 3 leaves or so, finger length, and again tie in any longer main growth you can reach. Feed with rose food in early June. (See **May**.)

PLAN VEG PATCH Digging time is here again – is it ever not? A few bags of compost tipped on the veg beds and dug in gradually, except for root crops for some reason. On cold dark days sit and plan what to plant where this year. Expert opinion says you should try for a 3 year rotation of the three main veg categories, in order to avoid disease from planting the same thing in the same bed every year.

The categories are: **Root Crops** (*Potatoes, carrots, celery, celeriac, leeks, beetroot.*) **Brassicas** (*Cabbage, spinach and salads.*) **Legumes** (*Peas, beans, onions.*) Or, more simply: Potatoes, brassicas, all other veg. Just move them around one bed, or one site, every year, and if possible come back to square one every three. My principle is plant something you can easily grow, can't easily or cheaply buy, or which tastes better grown yourself.

SEED POTATOES Believe it or not, now is the time to buy them, lined up in all their variety in the garden centre. New to vegetable gardening, I find them a doddle. Best if you can find them loose, as they are in my local garden centre, Courtens on the A27 on the way to Romsey. Then I get a dozen of each, as I did this year, of five different varieties. I normally get 'Charlottes' for second earlies/salad potatoes, yellow, waxy, delicious new, with mint or parsley, but this year am trying 'Pink Fir Apple'', those knobbly creatures, 'Nadine', 'Swift', 'Yukon Gold' and 'Santé.' It's fun to experiment each year. (See **September** for progress report.) I let them chit, ie sprout, in egg boxes in the unheated spare room window, and when they've got a couple of inches of dark green sprouting, plant them outside six inches apart and about four inches deep in rows about eighteen inches apart, stacking up soil over them to protect against frost and prevent them turning green from the light. Do this again when they come through. Tradition says you should plant potatoes on Good Friday, or in late March onwards. (See **March /April**.) Then abandon them until they've come up, flowered and flopped over.

Dig up a forkful each time you want them. They are best straight from the ground. Each plant should produce ten or twelve spuds that actually taste of something. Invariably I find last year's rogue ones, missed when digging up, poking up quite happily. No harm done, eat those too.

Courtens Garden Centre, Romsey Road, Whiteparish, Nr Salisbury, Wilts SP5 2SD. Telephone 01794 884489. Owner is Chris Hiles.

TIDYING AND SPLITTING GRASSES This is the month to cut deciduous grasses to the ground, and split up. With evergreen grasses simply pull out the dead paler coloured growth underneath, but wait till they're in growth from April onwards to cut them back by a third, if they need it. (See **October**.)

SNOWDROPS This is the month for them too. One minute nothing but tiny blue-ish green spiky leaves poking up, the next drifts of them in full delicious whitery along the woodland verges. Enjoy them while you may – they are there for a short precious moment. Galanthophiles go bonkers for permutations and pay fortunes for one rare bulb, but the only slightly different one I have here is *Galanthus elwesii* – taller, a bit later, with a bigger flower. When they grow into groups and start to look a bit motheaten, that's the time to split them – 'in the green' – you do it about every five years. Dig up a clump, pull it apart with your fingers or a small fork, shake out about a dozen bulbs, and replant where you want them to colonise, with a little bonemeal.

The first snowdrops – brightest and best in these dim months.

DISASTERS I have just chucked away two cistus and the red-flowered hamamelis 'Diane' or witch hazel, which suddenly died. The bright pink cistus, 'Sunset', had been a huge success on the corner for 2 or 3 years, with mauve clematis 'Arabella' sprawling all over it, then it started to go sickly brown. The God of Gardening likes *Cistus x cyprius*, large white flowers with a maroon blotch, and finds it long-lived. Worth a try. It could be me, but perhaps some things just die young. So out they came, and here are three empty sites for inspiration. A failure = an opportunity.

CHAENOMELES These prickly unpronounceable fellows (kainomeles), hitherto known as japonica, are worth growing, and their waxy flowers are an unexpected delight in February and March: white, 'Nivalis'; scarlet, 'Scarlet and Gold'; and the apple blossom one, 'Moerloosei'. They can be trained up a wall or a fence, under a window, around a door, or rather messily just grow in a bush. They prefer a sunny position, I think. Their quince–like fruit can be made into an excellent jelly. Spur prune after flowering to encourage more next year.

INDOOR PLANTS… sorry, what was that? I dropped off for a minute. I am totally bored by most indoor plants, but confess a sneaking admiration for the gloriously vulgar amaryllis or for God's sake, hippeastrum – that flamboyant lily-like creature growing from a massive bulb, in shades of red, pink, stripes and white. They make good Christmas presents, and they're fine for one year, taking about six weeks to flower from when you start to water them. But it's also worth getting the biggest bulb you can find, loose, about a fiver, and sometimes they come back year after year, which I can never get the others to do. After flowering, feed them, put them away somewhere frost-free, and ignore them until you decide to have

My aunt Dawn's amaryllis, came back again for several years.

another go next winter. You may be lucky. I'm also fond of blue hyacinths indoors, although they always flop most dramatically, and *'Tête à têtes'*.

I came across a book the other day, *Perfect Houseplants*. Two of my least favourite words together. Perfect – impossible. Houseplants – dreary dusty things infested with white fly. As far as I'm concerned, the most perfect houseplant is a dead one.

JOBS THIS MONTH

- Carry on winter wash, as in Jan.
- Prune clems and wisteria.
- Plant lilies, except the Madonna lily. (See **April**.)
- Buy seed potatoes and chit in spare room.
- Cut down deciduous grasses and split if you need to.
- Split and replant snowdrops.

Crocuses on the College roundabout in Salisbury.

Daphne odora *'Aureomarginata' has a delicious sweet scent.*

Chaenomeles 'Nivalis' likes a sunny wall.

Chaenomeles 'Moerloosei' is like apple blossom.

'Polish Spirit' clematis and the green Cotinus coggygria.

Crocus tommasianus *self-seeded around the pear tree.*

Snowdrop Elwesii – *taller and later.*

Clematis 'Elvan' scrambling up an apple tree
– prune this month.

The dawn breaks a little earlier each day.

And the sun sets a little later – over Old Sarum.

March

All my hurts my garden spade can heal.

Ralph Waldo Emerson, 1803 – 1882, who also said:

To fill the hour – that is happiness. and *We are always getting ready to live, but never living.* and *I hate quotations.*

Mad March: better than Feb but not as good as April. A bridge between winter and spring: one minute big storms, snow flurries, sleet showers, hands too cold and ground too hard to work in garden, the next lilac in bud and a sunny day to tidy up and prune the roses. It's a good month for painting trellis and fences, and the lawn may be ready for the first mow. Take heart. The endless winter may soon be over.

2011

6th Striped bumble on pulmonaria.

8th Blackbird singing from chimneypot at sunset and sunrise

16th Pussy willow, fat, fluffy, yellow, viewed from train.

18th Suddenly, blossom everywhere, pale pink.

21st Hung washing out for the first time. First sleepy wasp.

22nd Blackthorn out. First butterfly – pale yellow. Ribbons of daffs in full flower beside ring road.

23rd Spring has sprung. Second butterfly – a peacock. Peach blossom starting to come out. Fleece at night.

24th Tiniest fuzz of green on plum – buds are swelling. Blackbird picking up beakful of grasses.

26th Clocks go forward.

28th Two 'Apeldoorn' tulips out: one red, one yellow. Lunch on sunny deck for the first time – Waitrose deli and a glass of rosé. Magnolias out in their full glory: white first then pink.

29th First ducklings, 4 newborn, paddling frantically against the flow of Avon.

31st Clematis 'Jackmanii' miracle: 3 new shoots from stump.

PRUNE EVERGREENS My cousin Sue taught me the March evergreen rule: wait until now, and with luck the new growth on the clipped branches will avoid the last of this winter's frosts, and have all summer to harden off before next winter's. But don't do it if it's frosty, and wait until June for boxes. So I prop the ladder firmly against the bay tree, take up long and short secateurs, and start clipping it into a shaggy pyramid. This can take several sessions, because as always half the job is getting down and clearing up the debris. Always leave time and energy for the stuffing of the plastic bags or the loading of the wheelbarrow. Nothing is more demoralising than coming out the following day and finding a load of crap everywhere. Fun to topiarise anything you can lay your clippers on, particularly yew, holly and eleagnus.

PRUNING ROSES March used to be the proscribed month for the major prune, but with warmer winters (ha!) and earlier sproutings, you might find the urge to get your secateurs out in mid to late Feb, but again not if frosty. Try to get them done by the end of March. This is your opportunity to cut the naked and now visible stems to the shape that benefits you as well as them. Unpruned, they will reach for the sky – get them to the level where you can see and smell them.

So cut climbing roses to a sensible, lower, fan shape, chopping out the dead branches, those growing towards the the middle, those pointing at the wall, or coming towards you and about to poke your eye out, one if two are crossing over each other, anything really weedy and weak. Then trim back the others by about a third, above an outward-facing bud, and each year try to prune to the ground one major old stem. This will encourage new

healthy happy growth. Brush off any new pink buds going in the wrong direction. Tie in main branches horizontally if you can, to encourage flowers to break out, with a figure-of-eight knot, ie cross the ends over, so stem can expand – don't just tie in a loop, or worse, tuck it in behind wire. I use Flexi-tie, a stretchy brown tie, available from garden centres.

Sun and light – this is what roses, and all plants (and all humans) need. In all pruning, try to clear the centre of the bush, to make a cup shape. Branches in the middle, in the shade, get no light, grow nothing, wither and eventually die. It's the same principle for everything. Us too. How are your innermost branches?

Bush roses are cut back in a similar way, main stems by about a third on average. Hybrid Teas are traditionally cut to knee high, or even ankle high, each spring, but the beautiful bronze 'Remember Me' didn't like that much, so I became kinder. (Update November: still flowering, had a marvellous year, now bosom high.) Ramblers flower on previous year's growth, so the main pruning is done in early July, after they've finished flowering. Tie in the growth they've made since, and trim that up a little, but don't prune them much, or you won't get any flowers this year.

After pruning, feed: scatter special rose food around their roots, lightly fork in and water if rain not expected. You do this again after their first (or only) flush of flowers, at the end of June, or in July. Drop your banana skins at their feet too, or in the planting hole; it looks revolting but apparently they like the potassium.

Above all, don't be afraid of pruning roses. You cannot harm them. They will respond enthusiastically to whatever you do to them. (See **November** for winter prune.)

BLOODY BINDWEED "How can I get rid of this?" asked a blighted friend. This is an eyes raised to the ceiling moment. There is no way of getting rid of bindweed except to DIG IT UP. I speak from bitter experience. When I came here the garden was infested with it. For a year I dug and dug and dug. I dug up the paeonies and painstakingly extracted the distinctive white bindweed roots from theirs, and when the garden was redone, I kept on digging. When a bed is empty, that's the perfect time. In an established bed, the roots of other residents can be so entangled that you may have to sacrifice them. The bad news is unless you can get rid of every single bit of white root, it will come back to haunt your dreams, but keep at it, and eventually you will conquer it.

You can kill the odd recalcitrant stem with Roundup. Twine it around a cane inside an old plastic water bottle with the top and bottom cut off, and spray. This will protect other plants near it. You can spray where it grows, but if the wind blows it onto nearby plants, they will die too.

Beware of strangers bringing gifts: make sure that any plant given to you has not come from a bindweedy garden. Be firm. Just say no.

CAMELLIAS Where to start with these glorious creatures? Glossy of leaf, bright of flower, pink, red, white or yellow, they cheer us in the dark months of winter and all through the spring. If you have acid soil you will be able to grow them into vast bushes covered in paeony-like flowers. To find out, check if they grow in other people's gardens nearby or get a soil testing kit. (PH 5 & 6 = acid, PH 7 = neutral, above PH7 is alkaline.) They absolutely hate lime, ie chalky soils like mine, or ours here locally, and will look sickly with bilious yellowy-green leaves from lack of iron. (Other things which must be on acid, or at a pinch neutral, include: Heather (eek), pieris, magnolias,

some lilies (check), and hamamelis (witch hazel.) In Camellia Alley, outside the back door, I have 7 survivors from December's Arctic winds. Potted in ericaceous (acid) compost, and facing west, their best direction, they still froze solid and the victims died from thirst. It's essential to remember to water them, when it's possible, and with rain water, not tap (too chalky.) All summer. Yes. If they dry out, they die, or at the very least the next year's buds drop off. I am much better at remembering this if they are all grouped together. They look fabulous with chipped slate around them, particularly in blue pots. My favourites: 'Adolphe Audusson' – red, and 'Jury's Yellow' – yellow and white.

Feed every couple of weeks, from March to the end of September, with Miracle Gro ericaceous feed, one heaped spoonful in 1 gallon of water, so you can feed and water at the same time. This will encourage multiple buds, most rewardingly, and turn any yellow leaves green. Plus, I have learned from Chris at Courtens Garden Centre, a couple of teaspoons of Epsom Salts three or four times a year replace the magnesium that Miracle Gro now omits from its mix. Prune after flowering. And the bad news? *See June and December* for the joy of trying to prevent sooty mould. And *October* for how to protect them through the winter.

PLANT THINGS, SPLIT THINGS The soil warms up in March, and this is the month to plant. Start with splitting some overcrowded perennials, ie 3 year old *Iris sibirica* and *Aster frikartii 'Mönch'*. You need two border forks and a sharp spade. Water first, then divide a clump into bits about 3" to 4" across – you may need to dig it out first and place on a compost bag on a hard surface in order to get a good purchase. The usual method is back to back forks, and gently push roots apart. If this doesn't work, jump up and down on the spade, or carve up with an old bread knife. Some plants, eg paeonies,

Split and Plant: 1. Splitting Iris sibirica, dig up after watering.

3. Chop up with old knife or back to back forks.

2. *Nice big clump.*

4. Make sure each bit has shoots and good roots, then replant.

get woody in the centre, so chop off bits of the new growth around the edge, each with a little bud showing, and chuck the middle away. Replant all new clumps in chosen area, throwing in a handful of manure and another of bonemeal. Water well, and continue to do so for the first year of transplant. There! Loads of new plants for nothing at all. This is also the time to move plants that are in the wrong place. Water before digging up a nice big clump with as much earth as possible, then shove into a ready-made hole, water again, and it may not notice. Allow yourself a trip to the nursery for what else you have on your list, but don't be tempted by bedding plants yet – it's far too early.

NEW CLEMATISES With three spaces to fill, due to one death ('The President', wilt), one space *(digging up the bamboo)* and one inspiration *(Clem texensis* 'Princess Diana' *so successful crawling over one lavender bush I thought I might get another, for another)*, Steph, newly arrived from Edinburgh, and I set off for Nightingales Nursery in Romsey with a shopping list. So far, so good. We returned with five, seduced by mauve and crimson beauties, and therefore having committed the gardener's sin of buying on impulse, along with three red oriental poppies and three mauve aubrietias. Oops.

Nightingales is a proper nursery, with polytunnels heaving with their speciality: clematises, climbers and shrubs. A joy to walk the aisles of properly labelled, mostly flowering, healthy clems, at much better prices than garden centres (£6.90 - £7.50), and to deal with such nice, helpful and knowledgeable people as Roger and the owners Graham and Caroline Farmilow. *(See Appendix re how to plant them.)*

Nightingales Nursery, Gardeners Lane, Romsey, Hants S51 6AD, telephone 023 8081 4350. Open 7 days mid March - mid June, Mon - Fri otherwise.

How to plant a new plant

(Experienced gardeners look away now) You see people on the telly just digging a hole and stuffing it in. Would that it were as easy. So:

1. Soak plant in its pot in a bucket of water for about an hour – or until bubbles stop coming up. You can do this while you're…

2. Digging a hole a bit bigger than the pot, adding a handful of well rotted manure and another of bonemeal, and loosening the bottom with a small fork. Water and let it drain away – what the God calls "puddling in."

3. When pot well soaked, hold in one hand and with the other bash bottom and sides with a trowel to loosen, and tip out, still holding.

4. Gently tease roots out from bottom and around edges. Or break up the bottom with your hands or small fork. If you don't do this the roots will continue to go round and round and not down and down. This job is easier when the earth is soaking wet and dripping all over your knees.

Planting a new plant: 1. Soak well then tip out.

2. Gently tease out roots.

3. Plant in hole a little bigger than pot, add bonemeal and manure or compost. "Puddle in" with water first.

4. Firm in, then water again.

5. Stuff plant in hole, at the same level as it was in the pot (but a few inches deeper for clematises), twizzle about to face the best direction, and fill in round the edges with John Innes No. 3 compost or manure, mixed with earth. Firm in with the handle of the fork, then your hands, then your feet, gently, water in well. For clems mulch with a 15 inch collar of compost or manure about 2 inches thick, and some slates to keep the roots cool. Don't forget to water new plantings for the first year. If they came with a label, tie it on.

THE BIG MARCH TIDY UP Ah the joy of a spring afternoon, and a great garden housekeeping job to do. All those shrubby things that are beginning to sprout, buddleia, spiraea, caryopteris, perovskia, can now be pruned back – the first two by about half, the latter two almost to the ground. The idea of doing it in the spring, rather than the autumn, is to give these late-flowering plants some sort of protection over winter. In March the new growth is less likely to be zapped, though you can't count on there not being frosts until the end of May. Go through the garden gradually, tidying, pruning, weeding and feeding with handfuls of blood, fish and bone, from now on referred to as BFB, tickling up the soil with a fork.

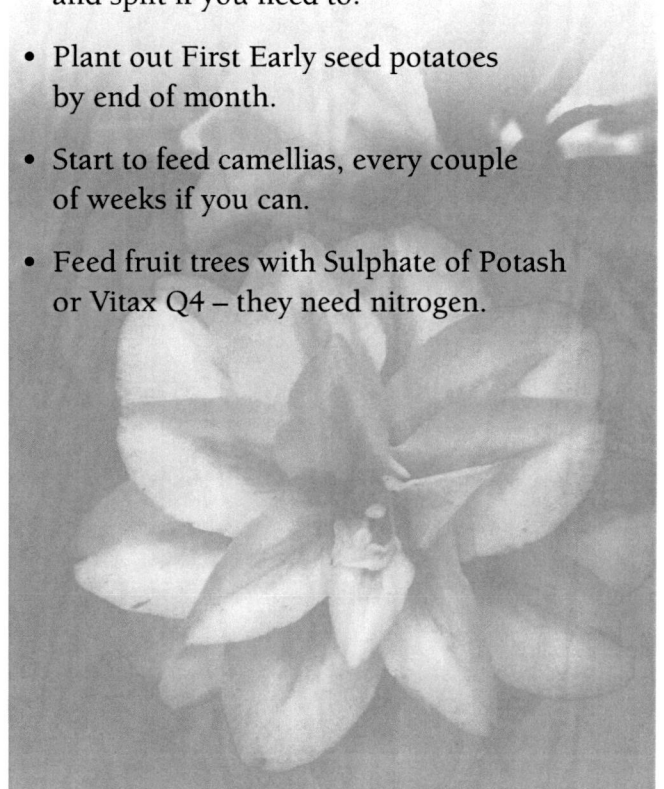

JOBS THIS MONTH

- Prune roses and feed.

- Last month to spray winter wash on fruit trees, unless buds are about to burst.

- Prune evergreens and lavenders. Trim an inch off lavenders. Don't feed.

- Tidy up garden. Feed BFB.

- Prune late-flowering shrubs: hydrangea, ceratostigma, caryopteris, perovskia, also penstemon, spiraea and buddleia.

- Sow seeds, indoors and out.

- Sow beans in cardboard loo rolls – indoors.

- Split and plant hardy perennials. Not if ground frozen: try digging a hole.

- Cut back deciduous grasses to ground, and split if you need to.

- Plant out First Early seed potatoes by end of month.

- Start to feed camellias, every couple of weeks if you can.

- Feed fruit trees with Sulphate of Potash or Vitax Q4 – they need nitrogen.

Very satisfying. Looks great afterwards, the soil has probably impacted over the winter, and rain can now sink in easier. Feeding tip: if you choose an afternoon where rain is expected, it will help the BFB sink in. Managed to do the whole garden in this way this year, scattering it about with big clouds overhead. And it has made a difference.

WE PLOUGH THE FIELDS AND SCATTER THE GOOD SEED ON THE LAND. Where are all those seeds you kept from last year, in brown paper bags, in a cool dry place? Oh no, they've not gone soggy, have they? Or the ones you fell for, in flatteringly photographed packets? Get 'em out and scatter. Some need doing indoors, like cosmos and single colour wallflowers. Eek, how I hate fiddling with seeds and seed trays, and worst of all PRICKING OUT. *(One of Monty Don's favourite jobs – well that says it all, really. When in doubt, prick 'em out.)* I hyperventilate if I see close-ups of Sarah Raven's fingers holding teeny weeny seedlingettes. I just have to grit my teeth and separate the little seedlings and prick them into tiny potlets. Vegetables are OK: I can do French beans in old loo rolls, and get down on my knees (buy foam kneeling pad) to plant spinach in drills outdoors. See **April** for more on veg.

Ribbons of daffodils by the ring road.

Yellow, the colour of spring. Scented daffodils from Cornwall.

Kingcups by the Avon.

Pussy willow, a sure sign of spring, down by the river.

Lunch on deck for the first time.

'Peregrine' peach blossom – happy on a west fence.

The superb magnolias in Queen Elizabeth Gardens.

Camellia 'Jury's Yellow' – one of my favourites.

'Elsie Jury' camellia – who was this Jury family?

April

Oh to be in England
Now that April's there,
And whoever wakes in England
Sees, some morning, unaware,
That the lowest boughs and the brushwood sheaf
Round the elm-tree bole are in tiny leaf,
While the chaffinch sings on the orchard bough
In England – now!

Robert Browning, 1812 – 1889. Home thoughts from Abroad.

'River's Early Prolific' plum blossom.

Now clocks have gone forward, I have to get up in the dark again. There is more gardening time in the evening, until around 6 the Arctic breezes begin and I have to retreat indoors and light the fire. It's officially spring: the trees are bursting into blossom, and I've never seen more primroses. Monty on TV is half useful and half ludicrous: plant potatoes on a layer of compost, sprinkle radishes or rocket seeds on top, good. Make a boiling barrel of "compost tea" at Wisley, with kits costing £600, and spend £3 on a grafted tomato – April Fool?

2011

2nd   Plum in froth of cream blossom. Sticky buds, chestnut leaves just unfurling.

4th   First bluebell spotted – two weeks early this year.

5th   'Apeldoorn Elites' out – yellow and orange stripy. What a family.

6th   Hawthorn in tiny leaf.

8th   Crabapple 'Floribunda' in glorious pink and white flower.

10th   Mauve wisteria out, white in fat bud.

13th   First 'Canary Bird' rose out in shady corner. First lilac lilac, purple to follow, white still in bud. Pink montana too.

16th   Pigeons constantly at it – great woo-wooing, today on roof. Yellow tree paeony in flower, and five babies seeded from last year.

19th   There goes the 7am heron again – perched on roof, scanning local ponds.

21st   White chestnut in flower, laburnum too.

22nd   Whitefly on boxes. Damn. Sprayed Provado Ultimate Bug Killer late evening.

26th   Pair coots and 4 cootlets on Avon. First 'Gertrude Jekyll' rose out.

TULIPS One day not there, the next in bud and then they're in coloured bud and then wowee…! Nothing beats the fantastic display, when the daffodils are tiring, and you're sick of yellow, and long for the smash hit vulgarity of oranges, purples and reds. No matter that so many fade away, it is worth it, worth it, WORTH IT. Buy more, plant more, note where you can shove in more, shove in lots. I planted 50 more yellow 'Golden Apeldoorns' last year, and 90 'Apeldoorn Elites.' I topped up my red 'Apeldoorn' bed with 100 more, and now there are so many it will be impossible to count them. Rapture. All the 'Apeldoorns' – Darwin Hybrids – increase yearly, excellent value. See **November** for planting. PS: Did I say it was worth it? (And no, I don't dig them up, but I pour liquid feed over them when flowers are over.)

CLEMATIS MONTANA: FRIEND OR FOE? Definitely friend, but yes, it can be a bit of a thug, this mad climbing clem. Once it gets stuck in, it'll be up that tree, over that roof, cascading over a fence like a waterfall, massively pink or massively

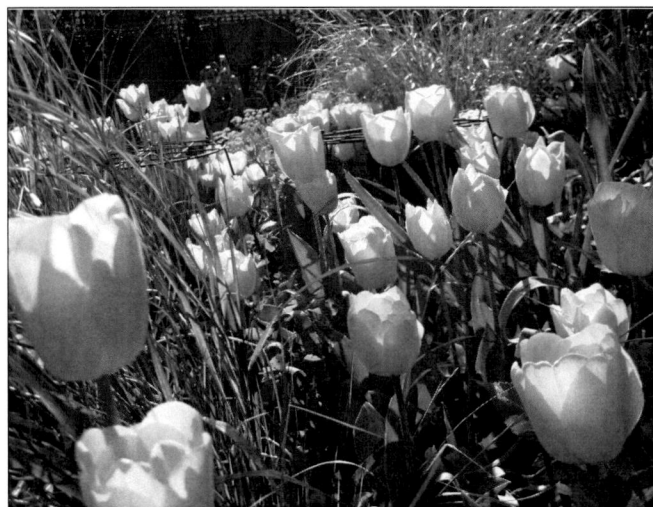

'Golden Apeldoorn' tulips and Stipa arundinacea.

white. That is the point of *C. montanas*. Like all clems they like shady feet and sunny heads. Give them sun, and space, that's all, and cut them back after they've flowered. Totally reliable, in bud at the beginning of April, and in prolific flower for most of the rest of the month, maybe into May. No garden should be without them. I have two unusual whites, 'Primrose Star' and 'Jacqui' tangled together over an apple tree.

OTHER EARLY CLEMATAE How welcome these early clematisses (what the hell is the plural, do you know?) are. *Clematis alpina* and *macropetala* are similar, delicate, small climbers with dangling bells in white, pink and shades of purple. I've seen a mauve one growing very effectively up a small obelisk in a tub, where it becomes a tower of flowers, and a white one, *macropetala* 'White Swan' growing up a pale green wall in the Close. Trim lightly after flowering, and again in February: like all early clems, they flower on the previous year's growth.

Clematis armandii is another thing altogether. With white waxy scented flowers, and evergreen shiny leaves, it is a very striking plant, but massively heavy and needs lots of space and really strong support, ie heavy wires on a house wall, or one dark night it might just blow down. Keep it under control, like *C. montana*, with a brutal haircut after flowering.

THE FRUIT AND VEGETABLE GARDEN Following on from Feb, where I suggested you start planning, now's a good time to think more about veg. If you have space, no matter how small, try filling it with something to eat. Or make a couple of veg beds. 4 feet wide is the usual recommendation, so you can reach everything easily, and simple treated gravel boards, nailed onto corner posts, make a good edging. Paths between should be wide enough to kneel on and wheel a barrow. If you have a west-facing wall, even with a bit of shade, how about thornless loganberries, which you can never get in the shops, but which do need at least 12 feet to stretch out their arms. Apple, pear and plum trees can grow almost anywhere in the garden, except in shade, and earn their space throughout the year, producing blossom and fruit. And even one red or black currant bush, or dessert gooseberry, is worth having. (My gooseberries have seeded themselves in the path. Baby, anyone?)

The beautiful early clematis 'Mrs P B Truax'.

Loganberries and dessert gooseberries – easy to grow, fruit in June.

ROTATION   As mentioned in Feb, try to move different categories of crops round beds every year. Remember **Potatoes, brassicas, all other veg**. "I think it could be a man thing", said my nephew Hugo, who has become a veg garden addict, and planted dozens of different ones. "Hunter gatherer."

GARDEN FURNITURE   Thinking ahead, it won't be long before you'll want to be sitting out there with a glass of rosé, so now is the month to spruce it up for summer. Or brace yourself and buy some, if you haven't got any, whatever you can find, and afford, and suits you and the house. Try the tip: people chuck this stuff away sometimes. Or boot sales, or weekly auctions. On my deck here I have cheap French folding café tables and chairs in blue, yellow and green stripes (Monoprix), another in red (Tesco, amazingly), and a pair of barn red wooden Adirondack chairs, cast off by Jenny's parents, which look totally uncomfortable, but amazingly aren't.

What have you all got? Nicky H-J and Sara C-B (this is the double-barrelled section, sit up at the back there), have faded teak, and the latter asked me what I would do with it, would I throw it away? Should she get cast iron? She has a big circular table with a hole in the middle for a parasol, and four very comfortable chairs. Extremely practical (though how many orang utans died as a result of felling the trees?), but sort of boring, faded and with a nice sheen of green mould. Um. But cast iron is bloody expensive, and a bit chilly. In the end, I suggested she paint them. Scrub them up, and try a couple of coats of woodstain. Not, please, one of the hideous diarrhoea shades, but a colour. Lots of people make outdoor stains and paints now, eg Sadolin, with a huge range, and Cuprinol, including Garden Shades, a water-based opaque paint, both of which I have successfully used. No prepping is needed, apart from the scrubbing-up, just slosh it on. They do protect the wood, as well as making it look so much friendlier. And you could brighten up with new cushions, too.

JOBS THIS MONTH

- Sow seeds of hardy annuals outdoors and tender ones, like cosmos, indoors.

- Keep splitting and planting hardy perennials.

- Plant French beans on windowsill, in tall coir pots or old loo roll innards.

- Think about garden furniture and scrub up for summer.

- Make a veg garden?

- Plant out potatoes: second earlies early April, maincrop mid to late April.

- Watch out for red lily beetles on newly emerging leaves. Squash, eek.

- Trim evergreen grasses, cut back by a third and split if you need to.

- Feed camellias every couple of weeks. Prune after flowering. Beware early scale insect – look under leaves. Spray Bio Provado Ultimate Bug Killer.

- Water pears when they flower: a bucket of water every week, before midday, as you still may have frosts in April. Carry on for six weeks – it helps them to fruit.

- Pour liquid feed over fading bulb foliage, to plump them up for next year.

COLOUR IN THE GARDEN (1) And following on furniture, let's think about the colour, not yet of the stars of the garden (see **August**), but of the supporting players of sheds and fences and obelisks and trellises and pergolas and pots and decks. Important as they are, a garden is not about all these, it's about flowers. So do we really want to be distracted by orange fence panels, or those bilious green pergola posts, the colours they become when tanalised? Eek, no, that looks a mess. I feel they should complement the colours growing up them, through them and against them. Designer Joe Swift's garden had black fences. Sounds dramatic but they worked brilliantly as a background to green frondy things, and I've just painted a pergola black too, very quiet and effective against the brick and black beams of a timber-framed house. A colour pulls a garden together, particularly if you have a hotch-potch of different sorts of fencing, rendered walls, sheds etc.

I am particularly fond of trellis. It's a pain in the arse to paint, best done before it's put up, both sides, right way up and upside down, two coats, but looks so much better when it's in place, its colour if possible matching the fence it's on. It's worth carefully choosing the colours of furniture, and pots too, maybe sticking to, say, terracotta and green. Or blue. Or grey. To use one of my most over-used phrases, it then looks like you've done it on purpose, rather than been the recipient of cast-offs.

BIRDS' NESTS, BEWARE How surprised I was to see a thrush hop onto my deck balustrade, with a beakful of worms, then fly up towards the pergola. And a few minutes later he flew down again, and off again, and back again with another mouthful. I had never seen a thrush in this garden before. He had expertly built a mossy nest on top of one of the horizontals, against the kitchen wall – an impregnable location (I hope) as it was right in the

middle of the thorniest rose of all time, 'Mermaid'. So now I have a family to raise I can't use slug pellets anywhere in the garden, even round the hostas. Daren't risk it. I couldn't be more excited to have a thrush, an increasingly rare bird, many of whose numbers have died out as a result of eating poisoned slugs and snails.

April of course is the prime nest-building month; it's forbidden by law to destroy a nest, so leave tree pruning and hedge cutting till later in the year, unless you're sure there are no nests. August on is safe, they say, some birds raising 2, if not 3, broods. In my neighbour's *leylandii* (cross yourself) there are two hedge sparrows and a blackbird nesting. Dad sits on top of the trellis, having stuttering hysterics when he spots Harpo, but mostly serenades me with the sweetest sound. A blackbird's song is so beautiful I could die listening and already be in heaven.

THE CANARY SINGS Walking out of the front door, on the 13th, I spotted 'Canary Bird', one of the earliest roses, like a splash of sunshine, in a dark north-facing corner. Small single yellow flowers are scattered over an untidy bush, about head height where I unkindly planted it, but at the front of Kate's house in the Close, on a west wall, it was enormous, occupying about 10 feet in each direction. Easy to grow, and I welcome anything which thrives in such an unprepossessing location. Above it flowers the purple lilac, a brilliant combination.

JENNY'S NEW "CHARLESTON CORNER" Summoned to Sherborne by my friend Jenny, who has a old terraced cottage there, with a good sized garden, we discussed what to plant in the cleared corner at the top right, next to an old apple tree, on a fence that faced south, and another west. An old lichened bench under the apple should have had

Virginia Woolf lounging on it, or Vanessa Bell, hence Charleston. We two lounged there and discussed clematises and roses, both of which would love the sun, provided we shaded the clem's feet. With Jenny poised to make a shopping list, The Voice of Doom spoke: "First you'll need to replace that fence which is about to blow over in the next gale, then you must have strong wires attached, and dig up a deeper, say 3ft, bed at the bottom, several times, to get rid of the brambles and ground elder. Then dig in bags and bags of compost and manure. Alas, infrastructure first, then the sexy bit." Preparation, as I've said somewhere else, is everything. Having done all this, in September she

could plant a climbing rose (say 'Compassion') on the right hand fence, and two clematises next March or April, when they are in good growth but not too tall to handle. Exciting choices for what to put in the bed in front of them: lilies, irises or a bush rose, like 'Yvonne Rabier' – small white clusters – which goes on and on flowering, and is in bud already (26th April) in my garden.

Jenny took it well. "I think I've moved on," she said, "from the impulse buying stage, coming home with all those expensive plants and not knowing where to put them, or that they'll grow so big. I'll make a list of everything that needs to be done." Yeay, Jen.

'Canary Bird' rose flowering in shady corner, out on 13th.

Clematis alpina 'Helsingborg' – small but beautifully formed.

'Apeldoorn Elites', out on the 5th. What a family.

Bumble bee in 'Floribunda' crabapple
– prettiest blossom, useless crabapples.

Coot and cootlets on the Avon.

*Laburnum and wisteria at Leena's B&B
on corner of Butts Road.*

Yellow tree paeony in flower on 16th, five babies seeded.

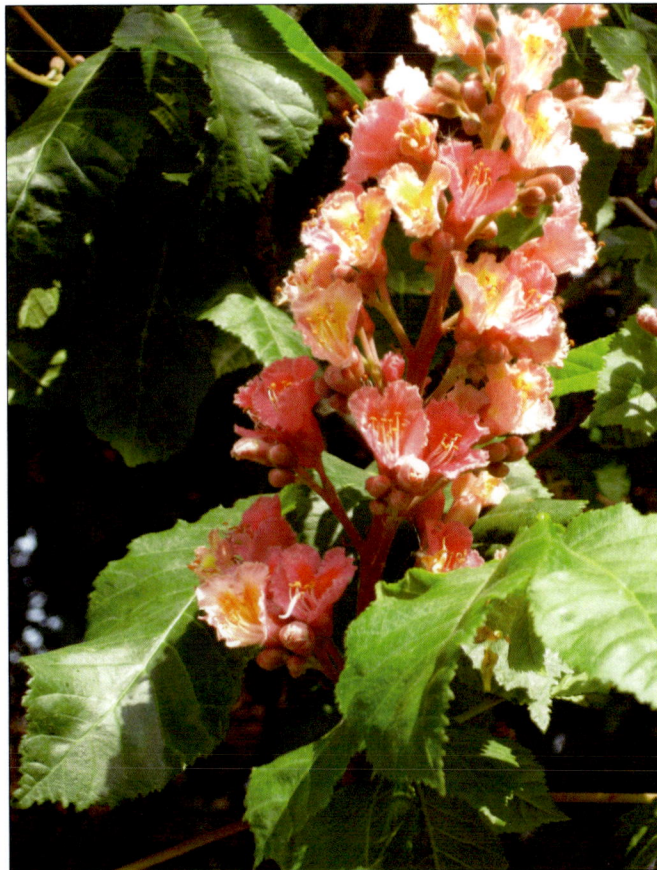

Pink horse chestnuts in glorious flower in Victoria Park.

*'Fire King' wallflowers, grown from seed.
Worth the pricking out.*

May

And after April, when May follows,
And the whitethroat builds, and all the swallows!
Hark, where my blossom'd pear-tree in the hedge
Leans to the field and scatters on the clover
Blossoms and dewdrops – at the bent spray's edge –
That's the wise thrush; he sings each song twice over
Lest you should think he never could recapture
The first fine careless rapture!

Robert Browning, 1812 – 1889. Home thoughts from Abroad.

'Arabella', a violet clematis that likes to crawl, not climb.

*M*onth of clear skies and empty Scottish beaches of white sand, with the gorse giving off the scent of coconut. Chestnuts in blossom, wisteria, laburnum, lilacs. Wood pigeons clumsily pursue each other, clumsily mate and build clumsy nests, and blackbirds perched on chimney pots are in a state of constant hysteria or ecstatic song. Month of casting a clout, then hurriedly putting it back on again. May at last.

2011

1st *Clematis montanas* flowering over the apple tree and hawthorns frothing over the hedgerows. All the whites.

4th Skylarks at Solstice Park – a vast moonscape dominated by Charlotte Moreton's landmark animal figures.

6th Rain at last. Ground desperate, water butts empty.

7th Swallows nesting in garden centre shed as usual. Red oriental poppy out. Cow parsley on verges, plus pink and white campions.

9th First philadelphus flower, dog roses in hedges.

10th 'Gertrude Jekyll', 'Variegata di Bologna', 'Compassion', 'Madame Alfred Carrière' roses out.

14th Swift shrieking over the garden.

20th Hollyhocks already in bud in Castle Road – what is going on?

21st Honeysuckle coming out at my bedroom window. You can put annuals out now, says old guy at market stall.

23rd First 'Leverkusen' and 'Wedding Day.'

26th First Flanders poppies in field by hospital.

27th First 'Mermaid' by bedroom window. Wood pigeons in last year's nest on pergola: fourth time lucky?

EUPHORBIAS When the world ends I guess the last plant standing will be *Euphorbia characias subsp.* 'Wulfenii'. Waist-high (or head high, in Jenny's garden) lime green flower bracts wave about in the wind, above rosettes of bluey-green leaves. They grow almost anywhere, and have a prehistoric feel – you almost expect a dinosaur to come whiffling through them. A smaller euphorbia (*amygdaloides?*) grows on unpromising ground on both north and south sides of a fence, the acid green making a startling contrast to the bluebells. When the flowers are over, cut them down at the base, being careful not to get the white sap on your hands – it can irritate. The leaves at the bottom will throw up next year's growth. If you want it to seed, leave one flower intact. Some I let grow where they fall, even at the front of the bed. Highly recommended, a most useful plant. I've tried to grow the rather glamorous reddish ones, *Euphorbia griffithii* 'Fireglow' and 'Dixter', without much success. As with so much, they either work or they don't. Philosophical thought of the month.

SECRET SUPPORT Give newly poking up multi-stemmed perennials a helping hand now to stay more or less upright, before they flop over in a despairing heap. I favour the circular plastic mesh with three legs, and a gentle feeding through of things like paeonies, phlox, gaillardia and Michaelmas daisies. The supports disappear completely once things are out. This year I discovered iron semi-circular hoops in Mompesson House garden (Salisbury, NT, recommended.) They are brilliantly holding up the echinopses and cephalariae, which normally collapse dramatically and have to be lashed with ropes. Canes are necessary for single stem plants like lilies, eryngiae, delphiniae and hollyhocks. Secret is the name of the game, saith The God of Gardening.

PAEONIES – A DELIGHTFUL DISCOVERY When I started on the jungle here, I suddenly spotted some new pink shoots poking up through a carpet of St John's Wort. They turned out to be the big double cottage garden crimson paeonies, *Paeonia officinalis* 'Rubra Plena'. The books say they hate being moved, but I dug them up, disentangled the white bindweed roots (see **March**), replanted them first in quarantine in pots, and later at the bottom of the garden, where they have flowered ever since. The secret I gather is not to put the corms in too deep – about an inch– and to plant in autumn, somewhere sunny. They split up quite easily, and it does them good to do this every eight to ten years. BFB them in the spring. There is also a bright pink 'Rubra Plena'.

Paeony flowers only last about five minutes, but how flamboyant they are. The first to come out here, in early May, is a fuchsia single one I bought so long ago I can't remember what it is. And a fluffy

My anonymous single paeony, out first, flowers last about 5 minutes.

double white one, 'Festiva Maxima.' I train them all through the 3-legged supports mentioned above. These and the paeony came from B & Q – a hit and miss place, they treat their plants abominably, but it's sometimes worth a look. Kelways in Somerset are the best. **Kelways Plants Ltd**, Barrymore Farm, Picts Hall, Langport TA10 9EZ, telephone 01458 250 521 www.kelways.co.uk They also specialise in tree paeonies, irises and ferns.

LABURNUM I love laburnum. I know it's suburban, but hey, I live in the suburbs. Its dripping racemes (good word) of sizzling yellow are dazzling against the blue sky, clashing superbly with pink may. I bought a tree when I redid the front garden, which took a while to get going, not helped by the snails slithering up the trunk and eating the leaves, damn them. This year, however, it flowered impressively in its fountain of yellow. When I remember I tip bucketfuls of bathwater over it. Worth struggling, I think, with one of the prettiest flowering trees. Needs a strong stake – it's tall and whippy.

Landford Trees, Landford Lodge, Landford, Salisbury, Wilts SP5 2EH. Telephone 01794 390808, www.landfordtrees.co.uk I also got many of my fruit trees from them.

ROSES (LATE MAY) Boy, so many already in flower this year: The first tender growth tends to attract greenfly, so I may give them one burst of Bio Provado Ultimate Bug Killer now, to kill this first attack while they are new and vulnerable, and let the ladybirds do their job the rest of the year. Similarly, I give them one blast of Fungus Fighter, as blackspot reappears, and hope they're strong enough to keep healthy until the autumn, when I think they all succumb, one way or the other. You can use up the rest of the fungicide on the hollyhocks, to try to prevent rust, a pretty hopeless task.

WISTERIA HYSTERIA Come over, do, in the middle of May (late April this year 2011), and admire one of the great sights of Salisbury: a Niagara Falls of white wisteria cascading down the west side of the house and dripping through the pergola below. Don't ask, no idea, complete fluke. My brother Julian gave it to me as a moving-in present in 2001, a family tradition, so I brazenly requested a tall one, to save waiting years for it to flower, and planted it in a small shallow bed. It immediately took off and now, 10 years later, not only covers that west wall but comes round the corner to the south, and is even making headway on the north. Every year it has more and bigger flowers, their scent wafting around the back of the house. It climbs over the upstairs windows, and up the chimney too, which means every year in late summer I have to stand on a ladder, poke my head through the pergola, shut my eyes, and heave it down. It does need pruning properly in order to flower (see **August** and **Feb**) and you can't do that if it's way up there. After pruning I tie it in to where I want it to go next. And feed it, with rose food, in early June.

Wisteria hysteria – a Niagara Falls of W. floribunda *'Alba'.*

'Compassion' climbing rose.
If I had only one in my garden, it would be this.

'Variegata di Bologna' raspberry ripple rose,
going bonkers this year.

'Gertrude Jekyll' rose racing up an obelisk:
one of the scentiest.

JOBS THIS MONTH

- The Chelsea Chop. Round about the time of the Chelsea Flower Show try cutting later flowering perennials, like sedum and perovskia, back by half. This encourages lower, bushier growth, a little later.
You can also do this as late as June or July.

- Support multi-stemmed perennials like paeonies and phlox.

- Feed lawn with Ecomix and BFB (See **September**.)

- Feed camellias every couple of weeks.

- Plant tender annuals (eg geraniums) at end of the month.

- Plant wallflower seeds in individual colours, indoors or out.

- Plant potatoes, if not done last month.

- Plant French beans on windowsill in tall coir pots or old loo rolls. Don't plant out till June – but if they've got going take them out for a while each day to harden off.

- Lightly prune early spring clems.

- Prune kerria, forsythia and chaenomeles when they've finished flowering.

- Spray roses with Fungus Fighter and Bio Provado Ultimate Bug Killer.

- Trim evergreen grasses, cut back a third and split if you need to,

Mine is *W. floribunda* 'Alba', and there are numerous others, apart from the familiar pale mauve *W. sinensis*. These in particular this year are so wisteria hysteria I screech dangerously to a halt to photograph them. The white one flowers slightly after the mauve – as I saw on Monet's Japanese bridge at Giverny, a wisteria "tunnel of vanilla" of both colours. They must must have sun, in order to flower. This year too they are out at the same time as the pink *montana* – a beautiful duo. God is good.

BLUE BLUE BLUE Christopher Lloyd, our late, much-beloved mentor, of Great Dixter, and Claude Monet, our even later, much-beloved mentor, of Giverny, loved blue and lamented the little of it there actually was in a garden. True blue, not "blue" as in so many optimistic descriptions of mauve. Blue like bluebells, blue like that salvia, a deep royal blue, blue like *Ceratostigma* in September, gentian blue, agapanthus, delphinium and anchusa blues, and here we are, at the end of May, with sudden deep glorious Ceanothus 'Concha' blue. That's what the big blue is, as you drive by, the first ceanothus to flower, the rest following on in June. There are dozens of varieties; be careful to get the right one, the right size, the right blue. Some grow into trees, some, beware, like 'Concha', into giant bushes. They look wonderful against a brick wall, but it must be a sunny one. Trim after flowering, but not too brutally – it doesn't like its old wood being cut into. I managed to kill one this way: it got so enormous I had to remove a few branches. All the leaves turned a bilious greenery-yallery and dropped off. Shit happens.

AND SO TO PHILADELPHUS If I had to make a Best Flowering Bush award, I would find it hard to choose between so many stunners that are out in May. Not content with the aforesaid lilacs, laburnums, may, and ceanothus, philadelphus is about to burst upon us in all its virgin white glory. Its delicious flowery scent floats at you from afar – the only thing in the garden my asthma-prone cousin Sue can smell. Chop off a few branches and bring them indoors to stink out an entire room. Mock orange blossom is its other name. There are single ones and double ones and ones with lime-green leaves, but Keep It Simple is my motto, and *Philadelphus* 'Belle Etoile', single white with a rose-pink heart, cannot be beaten, I think, and is readily available. I tried the lime-green one, P. aureus, but its ratio of flowers to leaves was pathetic, and became a great big lime green blob. Prune after flowering.

ALLIUMS Try filling a bed with *Allium cristophii*, a mauve catherine wheel on a tall stem, and if you fancy it you can pick them off when they dry and spray them gold *à la* Sarah Raven, sorry, I just fell asleep, for your Christmas table decoration. *Alliums (allia? alliae?)* are dramatic discoveries, from the onion family. 'Purple Sensation' is another good one, comes out slightly earlier, and will self seed. *A. giganteum* starts gigantic, but shrinks. Plant bulbs in November – they succeed tulips, and can be stuffed in at the same time.

Allium cristophii, with Knautia macedonica in the background.

CLEMATIS PROBLEMS Last year the dreaded clematis wilt hit 'The President' and 'Perle D'Azur'. 'The P' was growing strongly, then stems suddenly drooped, and the other never really got going. The clematis nursery, Nightingales in Romsey, advised cutting out wilted stems, or cutting down completely, if wilt is obvious, and water copper fungicide over whole plant and earth at the base, and they may regrow. Don't hesitate, they said, as wilt is a whadyacallit virus? that is airborne.

So I did, and in June 'The President' was flowering on the unwilted stems, and 'Perle D'Azur' was totally revived, with lots of new shoots coming up from the bottom. I had to tie it in almost daily. Alas, this year Death of a President, but 'Perle' shooting up again. Write it off to experience. The new vicar at St Martins here is a mad clemophile: he has 40 and swears by the *viticella* family; who could disagree? "I had 100 in Devon", he confessed. "I have a weakness for them."

Two Clematis montanas *on an old apple:* 'Primrose Star' *and* 'Jacqui'.

Raffy Moreton and his owner Charlotte's landmark horse at Solstice Park – stunning animal figures.

'Matador' *oriental poppy: if you've got it, flaunt it.*

'Madame Alfred Carrière', *an elegant, beautiful, scented and well-behaved climber. What more could one ask?*

CLEMS IN POTS Yes, you can, 14" diameter minimum, cover top with slate or similar, stand on bricks or pot feet, and water every day with 3 – 4 litres (half a 9L, 2 gall watering can.) Feed fortnightly with Tomorite, before they flower, and when they're in flower, with a general plant food, until they've done. Or stuff some Osmocote long distance pellets into the soil. So far so good with yellow *C. orientalis* 'Bill Mackenzie' on my north front wall. Prune in Feb, as usual.

Purple lilac, old-fashioned, fragrant,
one of the loveliest flowering trees.

How not to garden: an epic tale

From Steph in Edinburgh, via email

"Anemones de Caen, who could resist, white and pink. Picked up three, on a whim (*mistake number 1.*)

Sought out some bronze fennel. Only one left. No matter how many times I've said to myself don't buy one ONLY ONLY buy three, I once again managed to ignore myself (*mistake number 2.*) I did want it for the re-design in front of the rose, to add to the white foxgloves, the ruby astrantia and a paeony.

The beautiful whimsical anemones looked titty, totally titty, in WHATEVER position I put them in the border.

I eye up the unsatisfactory trough (*mistake number 3.*) I dig up the roots of the thing that failed in the snow, I plant the anemones and the fennel. They look rubbish. Sigh.

I eye the nice terracotta pot which has never been cleaned, only emptied of its contents recently, campanula, which arrived by force of nature. Pot into kitchen and given a right scrubbing. Out I go, broken pots in the bottom, good dose of lovely soil nicked from Paul's newly prepared sweet pea bed. Bronze fennel in the middle, anemones round about. TA DA.

Now where the hell to stand it. Hope no-one was watching as I put it there and put it here, and over there, in out, in out and shake it all about. Many spots later it's back to the place, of course, where I first put it."

June

I sing of brooks, of blossoms, birds, and bowers;
Of April, May, of June, and July-flowers.
I sing of maypoles, hock-carts, wassails, wakes,
Of bridegrooms, brides, and of their bridal cakes.

Robert Herrick, 1591- 1674. Hesperides, The Argument.

June at last: prime candidate for the best month of the year. Month of plenty; sudden glorious chaos in the borders, sudden dramatic collapse in the rains, much cursing, staking and tying in. The roses that came out at the end of May are getting into top gear, and the others follow. An embarrassment of riches. Drag out the loungers, you may even get a moment to sit and enjoy it. Raspberry smoothie lolly, anyone?

2011

3rd First hot day. Slather on the factor 30. Picnic at Old Sarum. My birthday.

5th Rain at last, after weeks of earth cracking drought. All roses flopped over.

6th Starting to graze gooseberries – they're colouring up.

8th Honeysuckle in flower – its honey scent hits you as you come round the corner.

10th Titchmarsh's new programme: *Love Your Garden*. Gardening for total morons. Yellow jasmine (*Jasminum humile* 'Revolutum') out. Also red hot ps.

13th First *Aster frikartii* 'Mönch'.

16th First *Lilium regale* 'Album' out.

19th Opened back door to pattering on gravel, fat hedgehog beating a fast retreat.

20th First clem 'Tangutica' out, yellow bells. Also purple 'Jackmanii'.

21st Longest day, Summer Solstice. Calling all druids, catching the Stonehenge buses in the rain. Calling all gardeners: lightish till 10 – are we still out there?

DERBY DAY TOPIARY Now is the time for all good gardeners to prise themselves out of their deckchairs, grab the scissors and sheep shearers and start clipping the boxes – *Buxus sempervirens*. No idea why Derby Day. It's the 4th this year. As I go I am also stuffing long bits, minus bottom leaves, cut off just below leaf node, into rooting gel, and then into a pot. They take easily, and the hedge I am now doing is composed of five to six-year-old cuttings, which have reached about a foot and a half, and joined up nicely. Numerous two-year olds, about 6 inches tall, have been planted as a putative hedge at the nursing home at which I now work as a volunteer gardener, Braemar Lodge. It is hard to resist rooting cuttings when you are chopping them off in such profusion.

POTTED BOXES On the deck are pots of boxes, clipped into balls, pyramids, cubes and a few combinations. Plain green or variegated, they are much slower growing than the ones in the ground, and need lots of food and water. Try Osmocote every six months, or Tomorite every couple of weeks in the summer, and pour the washing-up water over them too. With a huge tangle of roots, they need repotting every couple of years. As Kermit says, it's not easy being green, but as evergreen geometric shapes they stylishly dress up a deck or terrace throughout the year, when not much else is around. My godson Sam came up with the brilliant idea of scattering the blue and white shards I constantly find in the garden over the surface of the soil. It looks great, and makes watering easier. Slate chippings are a good alternative.

SECOND THOUGHTS ON ROSES I used to think roses were boring. Those stiff Hybrid Teas exhibited by old men at garden shows, those messy rose beds of multicoloured black-spotty bushes, still witnessed by Exeter Street roundabout – deadly.

Then I saw a friend's scarlet climber splashing over a garden wall. That was it – a totally different animal. When I moved to Salisbury, I found two climbers in my first garden, which I later identified as 'Compassion' (salmon pink, smelly, dark green leaves) and 'Leverkusen' (lemon yellow, lemon scented.) It was a slow burn love affair. Coming back from a Swiss holiday the first week of June, I opened the French doors and there was a mass of flowers, luminous in the evening light.

Beautiful roses: 'Leverkusen' climber goes a treat with purple Clematis 'Etoile Violette'.

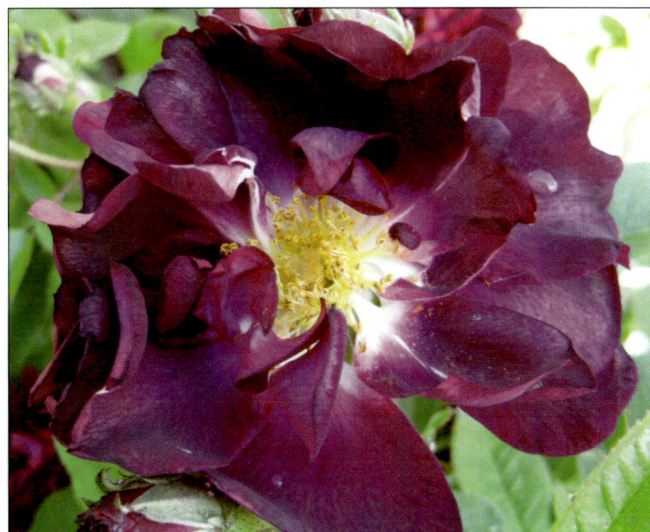

'Tuscany Superb', a once-flowering Gallica.

The rose that Steph gave me: 'Bonica', goes on and on, here tangled with 'Elvan' clematis.

Bumble in an unknown Mottisfont rose – they could improve their labelling.

The startling scarlet of 'Scharlachglüt', its moment brief but glorious.

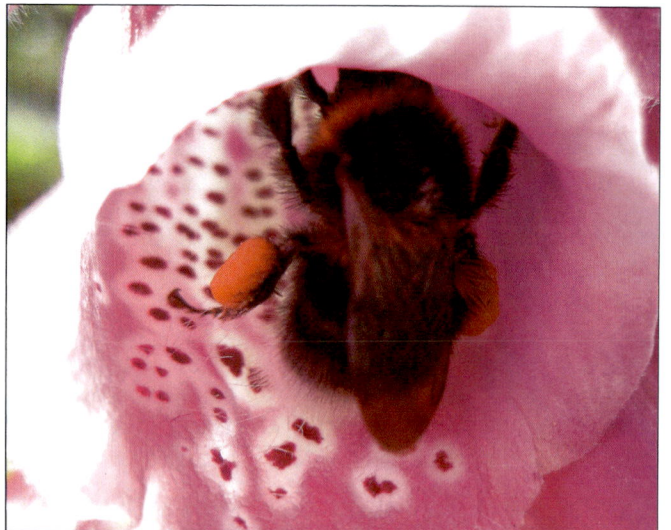

Bumble's bum in a foxglove – just shake about after they've flowered.

Now my garden here is full of them, many hitherto unknown to me, chosen by Steph in Scotland, when I described the space where I could squeeze another in. She is brilliant at rose research projects. She chose 'Variegata di Bologna', a raspberry ripple Bourbon rose, going completely bonkers this year, 'Tuscany Superb', a deep purply-crimson velvet *Gallica*, to fill a space in front of the bay tree, 'Yvonne Rabier', a small white constantly flowering rose, and, gloriously, 'Scharlachglüt', an exotic blood red climber. And I forgot 'Madame Alfred Carrière', a beautiful fragrant white rose with two or three flowerings per season, racing up the pergola. Steph started the whole thing off by giving me 'Bonica' when I first moved in: a utterly reliable pale pink modern shrub rose, which goes on and on. This year we have added 'Bright Future', an orange climber, on the fence where the deadly bamboo used to be. Nauseating name: we rechristened it *'Méthode Champenoise.'*

Mottisfont rose garden, a Must Go in June.

Oxeye daisies and 'Remember Me' rose – given to me to remember Faith Hillier.

Why are there so many terrible names? Pococks Roses catalogue gives us such treats as Mum's Blessing, Sweetie and Dick's Delight. Pass the sickbag, Nora. All these beauties are out now, as I write on 5th June, ridiculously early this year. "If I were cast away on a desert island," said Sara R-T the other evening, "I would ask for a basket of rose petals, to dig my nose into and breathe their glorious scent." We were standing by 'Gertrude Jekyll', one of the scentiest, winding her way up the new blue obelisk to explode at the top into a mass of bright pink flowers. I am drying those petals to make confetti for my cousin Miranda's wedding. The scent of *pot-pourri* as you go into the bedroom where they lie is delicious. I get all my roses from **Pococks**, in Romsey, just beyond Hilliers Arboretum – helpful and highly recommended. Jermyns Lane, Romsey, Hampshire SO51 0QA. Telephone 01794 367500. sales@pococksroses.co.uk

Near Romsey too, we are lucky in Salisbury to have Mottisfont Abbey, with Graham Stuart Thomas's National Collection of old roses. Go go go, any time in June, I went on the 2nd this year. Take a picnic, and walk through the beautiful grounds, where the Test trout river meanders, to the walled garden. It's always inspiring. They have several tearooms, a shop and the loos aren't bad. My friend Sarah and I sat and sucked ice creams in the courtyard and plant centre, accompanied by a pair of optimistic chaffinches. Not cheap, I'm afraid, (£7.60) though you can visit the abbey too. www.nationaltrust.org.uk/mottisfont.

THE WILD BUNCH Monet kept a special area at Giverny for his beloved rose bay willow herb, and allowed many other wild flowers to grow there. In the age of formal and funereal French gardens, as ever he led the fashion by at least 100 years. Who can resist bluebells, primroses, oxeye daisies, red Flanders poppies, herb robert, cow parsley, and foxgloves? The great thing about wild flowers is they're so tough, they grow well, nobody eats them and insects love them. Don't let them take over, though.

A FEW RUDE WORDS ABOUT POTS AND BEDDING PLANTS

The annual annuals rip-off is upon us. It costs a fortune to stuff your garden with them, unless you grow them yourself. I worked out I needed £100 worth of tobacco plants for my 'Apeldoorn' and Alliums bed, totally ridiculous, as you pull them out at the end of the summer. Don't get me started on why the Council don't save money by using more perennials, and fewer effing busy lizzies and tagetes and red salvias and petuniae and what are those poking up things called, hang on… cannas? I told you, don't get me started. Not to mention the appalling colour combinations.

Where were we? OK, if you must, a few pots of geraniae and blue dangling lobeliae, the classic combination, will be tolerated. As with all pots, the upside is that they're there, outside your door or window, to cheer you as you slave over last night's washing-up, and the downside is having to water them, probably daily. Keep them close to the house and, like the boxes, chuck your kitchen and bathwater over them. And feed them Tomorite. Put those dreary dusty houseplants out too and let them be rained on, or shrivel and die. R.I. bloody P if they do.

Still being rude, don't speak to me about hanging baskets, either. They need watering twice a day, for God's sake, and they're impossible to reach. OK for pubs perhaps: the baskets of yellow, orange and red dangling begonias I saw at The Boot, Houghton, a couple of summers ago were pretty damn impressive, if you like that sort of thing. This year they were red geraniums and blue lobelias. Good pub, The Boot, good food. On the river Test. Nicky and I had lunch there with her mad spaniels.

WATER IN THE GARDEN

This slight diversion to rant, pardon, brings us from hanging baskets to the ever-diminishing and increasingly expensive supply of water. What are you thinking, using the hose? It falls out of the sky, free. Install a water butt under every downpipe, and when it gets full prevent overflows, unless you have a gadget built in, by sticking a cork into the hole. I credit Malcolm B with this brilliant idea; sometimes they need a bit of shaving to fit. In addition, in warm spells, if any, put out every bucket and old washing-up bowl you possess, and collect rainwater. Another unconnected water butt is useful to tip it into. Or top up the pond. And what about shower water, bath water, washing-up water? A bucket in the shower can be tipped onto an apple tree, and several more can be generously watered with the bath water – *sans Occitane*, ideally. They say a new pear tree requires a bucketful every day in dry weather. Better one big watering than several little ones. OK to use a hose if they run out. Which they have (5th June.)

TOOLS

"Will you mention not buying expensive secateurs?" Nicky asked. Good idea, I said, I was going to mention basic tools. She had told me she was going to buy Nigel some secateurs for his birthday. "Don't get Felco," I said, "They're the best but not worth it unless you're a professional and spend all day pruning. Wilkinson make a perfectly good pair for £9.99, and get bypass not anvil mechanism, which stays sharper longer, in my experience, and in a bright colour, so you don't lose them."

So that is one essential. In addition I suggest: Pair kitchen scissors; long-handled loppers for fat branches; spade; fork; hand fork; trowel; rake; dustpan and brush; stiff broom; kneeling pad; wheelbarrow; watering cans, green and red; buckets; stepladder; lawnmower. Try to get tools in bright colours, or paint them if they're not. It's so easy to leave a trowel under a bush.

There's only one honeysuckle: 'Hall's Prolific'.

HONEYSUCKLE "There's only one," I told Jenny and Daphne, having tried and observed numerous in different positions, in different gardens. Some have handsome red flowers that don't smell, some run rampant, with few flowers, and have to be hacked back, some are shrubby ones, and worst, some go green with incurable mildew. When this happens they are revolting and the only thing to do is dig them out and throw them away. It's as much to do with the position as with the plant, says Helen Yemm, the *Daily Telegraph* gardening guru.* They like a sunny place with shade at their roots, rather like clematis, and won't thrive in a hot pot. Honeysuckles have such a lovely, old-fashioned appeal. To me, nothing beats the wild one, with its yellow and white flowers and fabulous scent. 'There's Only One' comes close: it has the same sort of flowers, the same sort of scent, does not get mildew, and is evergreen. It is 'Hall's Prolific'. Give it a try. It is now in glorious profusion (June 28th) and has reached my bedroom window, tangled up with the wisteria and the 'Mermaid' flowers.

*Helen has just had published *Thorny Problems*, an excellent book comprising her *DT* column problems, which my brother gave me. Knowledgeable and plain speaking. Recommended.

The Wild Bunch: bluebells in Grovely Woods, admired by Raffy, who's not at all wild.

HOW NOT TO GARDEN: AN AUTHOR'S TALE.
Oh yes, I have many a contribution to this slot, inaugurated last month by Steph in Edinburgh. When she was here I bought a crawling red *clematis texensis* 'Gravetye Beauty' for a spot under a lavender bush, along with several other red ones, some on my list and some on impulse *(mistake number 1.)* I soaked it for an hour while I dug a hole against the fence. And planted it there. *(Mistake number 2.)* Almost immediately I realised what I'd done, cursed, dug it up and it was so saturated half its roots fell off. *(Mistake number 3.)* I replanted at the bottom of the lavender and watched it slowly die. Oh dear, what a wanker.

The tabby hunter. Mice, beware.

OH THOSE SUMMER NIGHTS Calling the reluctant Harpo in around 10 on Saturday 25th, still lightish, I was aware of moths whirring and flitting, bats batting like jets overhead, tiny mouse squeaks, no doubt heard also by the tabby hunter, and intriguingly a scratching about in the paeonies. I could see nothing moving, but I'm sure it was the hedgehog. Here I was, living in a town, surrounded by the silent sounds of a summer night. Sometimes we just need to listen.

JOBS THIS MONTH

- Clip boxes on Derby Day or as close as you can.

- Cut euphorbias' flowered stems to the ground. Leave one if you want it to seed.

- Feed wisteria with rose food.

- Feed camellias every couple of weeks, and spray with Bio Provado Ultimate Bug Killer – under the leaves. This is the month for scale insect eggs to be laid.

- Plant out French beans.

- Plant bedding plants (if you must) now danger of frost is over.

- Trim evergreen grasses, cut back by a third and split if you need to.

- Dead head, dead head, dead head, so plants won't waste energy on seeds.

- Prune ramblers after flowering, then feed.

- Prune early flowering clems – *C.alpina, C.macropetala, C.montana.*

- Prune philadelphus and ceanothus, and any other just-flowered shrub.

- Watch Wimbledon and stuff the garden.

July

The English winter – ending in July,
To recommence in August.

Lord Byron, 1788 – 1824. Don Juan.

*L*ess *to spot coming out than going in. Roses are still flowering early July. The midsummer clems are in bud, phloxes are peaking, cephalaria is beaten down, roped up, and still a bumble magnet, and you can start digging up the first early spuds. With luck your French beans are twining their way up the canes, and the surviving courgette has grown leaves too hairy for snails. The July Slump is about to begin. Are we despairing? You betcha. Gird up our loins: late summer, here we come.*

2011

1st Mrs Blackbird feeding loganberries to two fat youngsters on the trellis. I am grazing gazillions of gooseberries. First plum eaten, my old tree 'River's Early'. About ten days early this year.

2nd First purple buddleia: 'Black Knight'. *Clem viticella* 'Elvan' a mass of purple bells for a week now.

4th Hedgehog visiting 6 am, snuffling about under the bird feeders.

5th Another, bigger, ditto. Have had to block up holes under fence to deter rats. Tropical downpours: heating back on.

12th Rowan weighed down with orange berries. Young blackbird eating the plums.

15th Red kite! Over in Berkshire. Apparently they are common round there.

17th Driving back from Miranda's wedding, yellow ragwort, knapweed, campions.

20th Hydrangeas (*hortensias*) in Normandy: banks of purple, crimson, bright blue.

30th First pear picked, 'Beth', and last plum.

"MY GARDEN FALLS APART IN THE SUMMER, WITH VERY LITTLE COLOUR. WHAT CAN I DO?" So asked Jenny of Sherborne. This is the nub of gardening, and the month to consider it. Summer is the time for perennials and annuals to come into their own. Here is a random selection spotted in the last few days (I write on 7th July):

Acanthus spinosus One of the infamous prickly gang, also popular with the poncers as an 'architectural' plant, not only for its striking upright mauve and white flowers, but also for its bold spiky leaves' appearance in classical carvings. Needs big semi-circular support before it flops over. *Aster frikartii* 'Mönch', of course, essential Michaelmas d. (See Appendix.) **Buddleia** big purple (see Appendix.) *Cephalaria gigantea*, big yellow scabious (see Appendix.) **Clematis**, all sorts (see Appendix.) **Crocosmia** red or orange, spiky leaves. **Eryngium**, or sea holly, subtly mauve spiky number beloved of bees. It needs one cane. Grow a group of 3 or 5 together. Mine are mostly *Eryngium planum*. Self-seeds. **Echinops**, big blue (see Appendix.) **Fuchsia** flamboyant flowering shrub, pinks, reds. **Fennel**, normal or bronze (see Appendix.) **Gaillardia**, gaudy red and yellow daisies. **Golden rod**, yellow (if you must, bit of a thug, the bloody thing seeds everywhere.) **Hardy geranium** shades of mauve or white, garden essentials (see Appendix.) **Hebe** (if you insist – a boring flowering shrub.) **Heleniums** 'Moerheim Beauty', rust-red daisylike perennials, yellow and orange ones too. Beware snails. **Helianthus** – sunflowers. **Hemerocallis** (day lilies) are lilies that last a day, amazingly. Useful plants in rich colours. Divide clumps every few years or they stop flowering. **Hibiscus**, exotic shrub with lavender blue or pink trumpetty flowers. **Hollyhocks** (*alcea*), welcome in all their colours, single or double, provided they don't wither from rust or the attentions of gastropods, which most of them do. They need a cane each, last about three years,

and self-seed. The odd flower might still appear into November. **Honeysuckle**, at its peak in July. (See Appendix.) **Hydrangeas** I'm in two minds about. Having admired the blue and purple ones in Normandy, due to the acid soil there, (see 20th July this year above) I am rather bored by the old ladies' knicker pinks around here, due to our chalk. These are *Hydrangea macrophylla* – the common hydrangea. **Hypericum**, **St John's Wort**, yellow-flowered bush, beware, can take over. **Japanese anemones**, white or pink (see *Anemone hybrida* in Appendix.) **Jasmine**, mad sweet-smelling climber with tiny white flowers. Hack back ruthlessly in spring. **Lavender**, garden essential. (See Appendix, later this chapter and numerous other places.) **Lilies** (see *Lilium regale* in Appendix.) **Marigolds**, yellow or orange. **Penstemons**, red, purple and pink. **Poppies**, Oriental, opium or any other, most self-seeding. (See Appendix.) **Roses** of course, though fewer in July. (See Appendix and all over this book.) **Sweet peas**. Try making a tunnel of them out of hazel rods, bending the top ones over long ones running lengthways. If it works, you can smell them from several feet away. The God recommends Grandifloras, including 'Painted Lady' for best scent. **Valerian**, red, white and pink, bit of a devil, seeds everywhere, paths, walls. *Verbena bonariensis*, mauvish flowers (see Appendix.)

Blimey, that's quite a selection. I never knew there were so many. Keeping colour going just needs a bit of thinking ahead. Keep it simple: decide on your favourites and plant generous numbers of them, 3, 5, 7, 9, not a spotty Smarties effect of one of everything. It is no sin to repeat plants in different parts of the garden, if you have room. Decide on a colour scheme and don't forget all year structure like evergreens, maybe clipped into geometric shapes. When you're happy with your summer garden, start to think about the autumn, and the winter. Same principles apply.

*Month of the clematae: 'Venosa Violacea'
and 'Romantika' growing together.*

*Clematis tangutica starts in summer and goes on till autumn.
Here with lobelia, one of the annuals I will allow in my garden.*

THE JOY OF CLEMATAE Got walls, fences, sheds, oil tanks, garages, old trees? Think vertical. Think clematis. They take up almost no space at the bottom and cover miraculously, with minimum attention, at the top. Flamboyant creatures; the more you plant, the more you learn how to look after them, the more they reward you. Especially in July, when so much else has gone over. With a bit of working out, you can have clems in flower nearly all year.

Start with the two monster winter ones (see **January**), *Clematis cirrhosa* and scented white waxy flowered *C. armandii*. By the time these are out the *C. montanas* are in bud, (see **April**), followed by the bell-like *alpina* and *macropetala*, and come June/July the *crème de la crème* of clems, the *viticellas*, are upon us, and also the crawling (as opposed to climbing) *C. texensis*. There are also some very handsome big-flowered July clems, like 'Marie Boisselot' and 'Lasurstern', but they can suffer from the mysterious clematis wilt, and suddenly, well, wilt, so I don't trust them.

So here we are in July with the numerous members of the said *viticellas*, the friendliest family of the clematis world. As you hack 'em back in Feb (see **February**) they take time to grow again, until wow there they suddenly are, a mass of bells or small

Close-up of 'Romantika', so beautiful I couldn't resist.

flowers, heads poking out of the top of a tree, or affectionately embracing a rose. My favourites are listed in Feb, and to these I add 'Romantika' with a k, deep velvety violet, and 'Venosa Violacea', purple and white, which I grow together.

And just when these are tiring, here come the *tanguticas* and *orientalisses* – a tangle of yellow bells, followed by fluffy flower heads like the native old man's beard. 'Bill Mackenzie' has taken off like a rocket, and is now up to the roof, good man. Still the odd flower in November and then here we are again with *Clem cirrhosa*. Go for it.

One of the loveliest lavenders, 'Twickel's Purple' – I couldn't do without them and they love our chalky soil.

My plum tree, 'River's Early Prolific', ripe in July, delicious, tangy, prolific – and how.

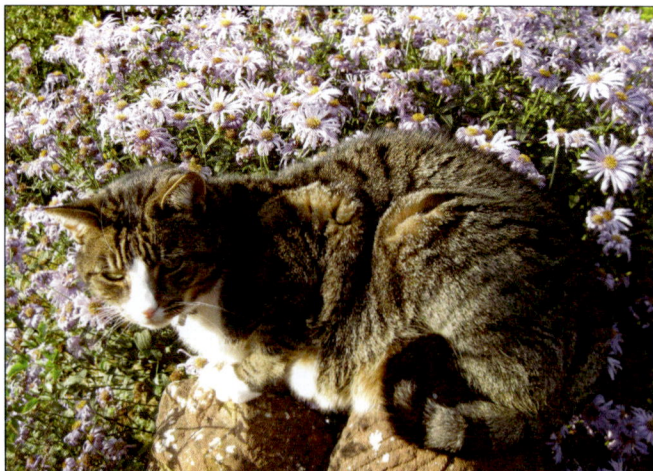

Harpo and Aster frikartii *'Mönch', starts in July, goes on for three months.*

LAVENDER AND ROSEMARY Survivors these certainly are. Hot weather plants, flourishing on the crappiest of soils on Mediterranean hillsides, they're equally at home in a British garden, as long as they have good drainage and lots and lots and lots of sun.

For lavender, buy the dead ordinary ones that are hardy, ie *Lavandula augustifolia* 'Hidcote' and 'Twickel's Purple', both deep violet, and that old stalwart, 'Munstead'. There's also a white one, which struggles a bit in my front garden, but which can still be out in October, and a pink one which is coming on slowly, though is not so tough.

French lavender, *Lavandula stoechas*, is lovely but a bit more doubtful in winter weather. Can be OK, or can succumb, take a chance if you really like it. Cuttings are easy: in August and September cut off a non-flowering stem, trim below a leaf joint, rip off lowest leaves, dip bottom in hormone rooting

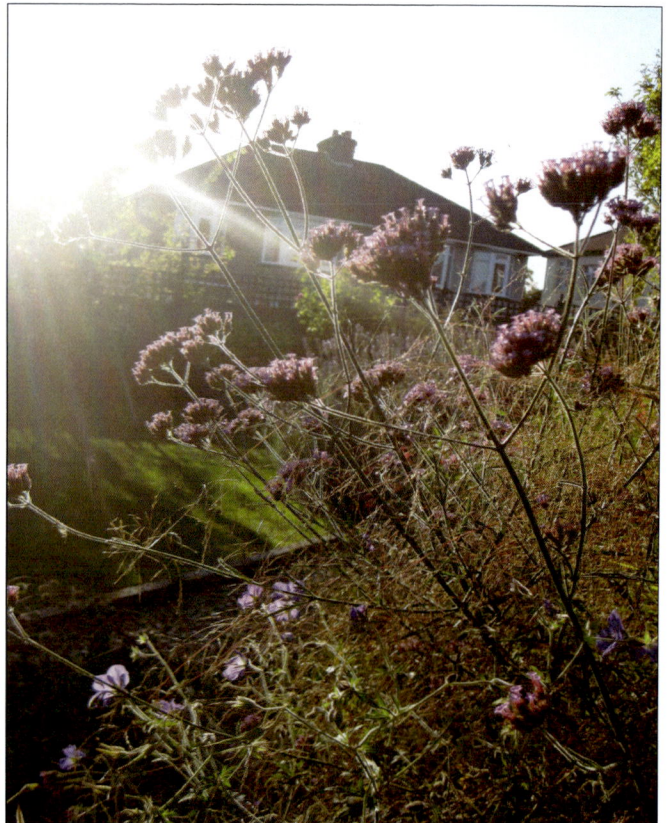

Verbena bonariensis, good with grasses, hardy geranium underneath.

powder or gel, and stick in gritty compost in a shady part of the garden, trimming top leaves a little. Most of them take (cough, update, only one survived this hideous winter) and by next summer will have grown into strong plants. Transfer into small pots in early summer. Prune first in August/September, (someone said on August Bank Holiday), when they've flowered, just cutting off their flowering stems with a pair of scissors. In March (see **March**) trim again, about an inch further down, being careful not to cut into the old wood. Then ignore. Do not feed.

For rosemary, all the above applies. The simplest, and most common, is *Rosmarinus officinalis*, perfect to snip off when roasting lamb. I also have *R. prostratus*, which the RHS Encyclopaedia says is the least hardy, but which has crawled happily down the Med Bed for some years. 'Miss Jessop's Upright', can grow to 6ft tall, but so far is short and obese. Prune after flowering.

READING ON A WET AFTERNOON For inspiring reading, there is nobody better or funnier or more opinionated than the late lamented Christopher Lloyd: try *The Well-Tempered Garden, The Adventurous Gardener, Colour for Adventurous Gardeners,* and, most difficult of all to achieve, *Succession Planting for Adventurous Gardeners.* That's us, OK? Lloyd's letters to and from Beth Chatto, *Dear Friend and Gardener,* are delightful. To me he is the Elizabeth David of gardening – remember reading her books like novels? I am currently reading *Cuttings* in the appropriate month of his gardening observations.

My essential reference book is the weapon of mass destruction, *RHS A-Z Encyclopedia of Garden Plants.* You can usually pick it up (just) in remainder bookshops for around £35, or second hand from Amazon for around £18. Haunt charity shops too for gardening books. Other favourite authors are

Oh dear, another bumble close-up: this is Echinops, a big blue late summer stalwart.

Yet another close-up of a bee, do I have a thing about them? In the huge scabious, Cephalaria gigantea.

Lilium regale 'Album', gorgeous scent, plant near sitting out area.

Roy Strong on garden design, Geoff Hamilton on anything, and anybody, with lots of pictures, on Monet's garden, Giverny. The Hessayon paperbacks on all subjects from Lawns to Flowering Shrubs are a cheap and essential part of a gardener's library.

THE STORE CUPBOARD Nicky has suggested I make a list of basic gardening stores, as well as tools (see **June**.) OK, this is what I have in my shed – how about you?

Compost (John Innes Nos 1,2,3 and ericaceous.) Bonemeal (packet.) Rose food (packet.) Manure – 2 or 3 bags, or 1 bag 6-X. Grit – one small bag. Blood fish and bone (BFB) in big tub. Hormone rooting powder or gel. Lawn spot weedkiller (spray bottle.) Fungicide (I use Bio Systhane Fungus Fighter.) Bio Provado Ultimate Bug Killer spray. Roundup spray. Plastic pots, assorted. Other nice ceramic and terracotta pots. Pot of old crocks. Labels, marking pen. Cane caps. Horrid green string (the nicer jute ones rot, alas.) Stretchy brown plant tie – Flexitie. Old manure/compost bags for rubbish storage. Jolly coloured plastic trugs. Buckets. Old washing up bowls.

THE BAD GUYS I suppose bad guys have a purpose, in growing so fast that they can cover oil tanks and hideous views – like the dreaded *Cupressus leylandii*. But they grow out of control so fast, so do beware: lysimachia, an attractive perennial with spikes of yellow flowers, spreads underground to take over the whole border; St John's Wort – hypericum – see list above – is another yellow peril. It quickly forms a big bush, or creeps along the ground, rooting as it goes. When I came here it had made an unholy alliance with the bindweed and their joint roots were knotted like carpet. Gardener's gaiters (*Phalaris arundinacea*) is another pest – a green and white stripy grass you'll

suddenly find poking up six feet away from where you planted it. And beware the pink Japanese anemone (see **August**.) As for bloody bamboo … a devil. Plant it safely in a pot so it can't escape and take over the world, invading your neighbour's garden as well as your own. But Public Enemy No. 1 is undoubtedly Russian effing vine: Do not on pain of death plant this smothering monstrous climber in your garden, or even I would say, move into a house where it is growing next door. Fortunately you can kill it with Roundup. Ugh.

JOBS THIS MONTH

- Keep pruning the ramblers, then feed. (See **March** for main pruning notes.)
- Feed all roses.
- Keep feeding camellias every couple of weeks.
- Prune rosemary after flowering.
- Feed day lilies with liquid feed – just pour over them.
- Sow wallflower seeds somewhere out of the way in garden, or in seed trays.
- Keep cutting back hardy geraniums. They will flower again.
- Water all pots daily if it's a hot spell, also young beans and courgettes and any other newbies, veg and apple and pear trees need water to ripen.
- Spray camellias, under leaves, with Bio Provado Ultimate Bug Killer, to destroy scale insect eggs. July is the month they lay them.
- Trim evergreen grasses, if you haven't already done so. Cut back by a third.

August

Our England is a garden, and such gardens are not made
By singing: – "Oh, how beautiful!" and sitting in the shade
While better men than we go out and start their working lives
At grubbing weeds from gravel paths with broken dinner-knives.
Then seek your job with thankfulness and work till further orders,
If it's only netting strawberries or killing slugs on borders;
And when your back stops aching and your hands begin to harden,
You will find yourself a partner in the Glory of the Garden.

Rudyard Kipling, 1865 – 1936. The Glory of the Garden.

Are we sitting here complaining it's too hot, or that it's another bloody useless English summer? Enjoy The Glory of the Garden this month. This is one of the reasons why we do it: on a warm evening to invite Angela E over for chilli and coriander prawns and a glass of rosé on the deck. How politely she admired the shambles around her – the fluffy pink anonymous rambler tearing at her skirt, the millions of tiny purple clem flowers cascading over the table. This, I said to her, is what it's all about. Cheers!

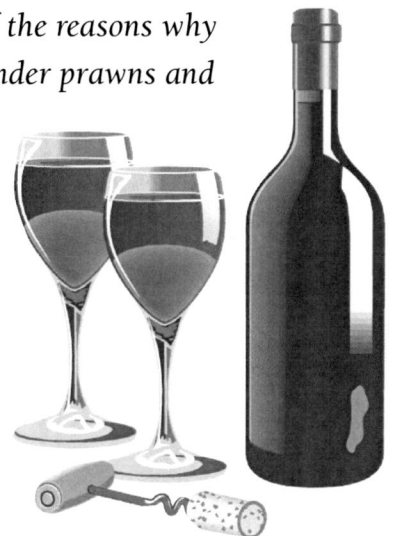

2011

1st First peach picked, 'Peregrine'.

6th "Caroline, can you use any damsons?" from Ann. I leave with 10lb and start jamming. Um, my favourite.

7th Heleniums golden, yellow, red striped all ablaze at Braemar Lodge.

8th Eating two or three peaches a day. Best year yet, after hideous winter. Even Rose and Andrew in Lancashire have 20 on their wall-trained tree.

10th Two young goldfinches still being fed by parents. Learn how, boys.

15th The robin's return. Where do they go all summer?

17th Picking handful of French beans a day now. Digging up main crop spuds. 'Madame Alfred Carrière' in full flower again all over the pergola.

19th Thrush bashing snail on stone: I watch, marvelling.

22nd Foggy morning, a few spiders' webs: autumn?

27th White *cyclamen hederifoliums* planted by Harpo's grave, who died yesterday.

31st Baby frog on back doorstep.

"WHAT'S OUT IN AUGUST?" Nicky asked me the other day. Most of what was out in July, and in addition: **Achillea**, tame relative of the wild yarrow, flat platforms of flowers, yellow, red, pink. **Agapanthus**, blue or white. **Caryopteris**, useful late season silvery-leaved plant, mauve flowers. Cut back in spring. (See **Appendix**.)

Ceratostigma willmottianum, blue. **Coreopsis**, huge range of yellow daisies – flag in too hot a spot. **Dahlia**, all colours, fashionable and effective if you can be bothered to dig them up or cover them up in the winter. **Echinacea**, prairie planting favourites of pink or white daisy-like flowers with prominent middles and downward-facing petals. **Lavatera**, big flowery bush, in a rather disgusting pink, or pale 'Barnsley'. **Nasturtiums**, old, reliable troupers, self-seeding. When in doubt plant a packet of the trailing ones over walls, across paths and up trellis. **Perovskia** 'Blue Spire' is most common. Silvery leaves. Must have sun. Try Chelsea Chop. **Phlox**, pink ones first, then white. Not too sunny a spot, OK even in shade. Water well and chop off flowered heads to encourage more. (See **Appendix**.) **Potentilla**, mass of small

yellow flowers on useful shrub. **Scabious**, any member of this family is worth having.

COLOUR IN THE GARDEN (2) Boy, take a look at a Salisbury roundabout and figure out what works and what so doesn't. Don't get me started on municipal colour schemes. The Salisbury ones make me wince. Purple, pink and scarlet together are fine, but they hang orange, yellow and blue baskets next door. Are they all colourblind? The God and my other gardening guru, Gertrude Jekyll, believed that no colour stands alone – it must be considered in relation to the ones beside it. The G of G wrote an entire book on the subject, *Colour for Adventurous Gardeners*, as mentioned last month, full of dazzling colour combinations. To get it right is a fabulous conundrum, and one to while away many a long hot afternoon. The fabled colour wheel tells us that colours work if they're either next to each other, or opposite. Purple goes with pink, or with orange; blue with purple, or yellow (my favourite combination.) But who gives a toss about the colour wheel? (See under municipals.) Try anything. We are adventurous gardeners, are we not? I've had the usual dog's dinner result with all of my carefully worked out colours, natch. No matter how hard I try, sure as hell a rogue will creep in and fuck the whole thing up.

THE RETURN OF THE CLEM The clematis I thought was dead two years ago, has suddenly reappeared. Last summer I was sitting resting between intensive weeding on the Gaudy bed, when I spotted something white and mauve at the bottom of the tepee, poking out of the geraniums. It was 'Venosa Violacea', resurrected. It then proceeded to climb up the rose, flowering as it went, and was still doing so in November. This year it has grown healthily. A miracle. Nil bloody desperandum.

Equally, after cutting 'Jackmanii' to the ground, nine stems have sprung up and there it is still flowering all over the fence. (Though rather mildewy this year, as is so much, due to drought. I have just emptied two buckets of shower water over it.)

WHY WE GARDEN: A SMALL MOMENT OF NAVEL GAZING Dutch researchers recently came up with the conclusion that allotments help people live longer. "Being outdoors, exercise, focus, help people cope better with ageing." The art of the bleeding obvious, if you ask me. And not just ageing: "The allotment has saved my life," Sara, an occasionally depressed friend recently told me.

I swear I will not disappear up my navel into the whys of gardening, but I do think being outdoors among other living things of which we are a part helps us all to live healthily, both physically and mentally. It helps prisoners, Nelson Mandela, the blind, people with learning difficulties. I like to be in the open air most afternoons, messing around, changing things, growing things, listening to the silence, and the blackbird, and the bees. And the

Heleniums come in rich colours, a late summer star, if you can save them from the snails.

Perovskia, another useful late summer plant. Chelsea Chop in May, give them some support. Must have unshaded sun.

Caryopteris 'Kew Blue' – a useful August to October perennial. Don't prune till spring.

Nasturtiums – plant a packet of trailing and let them rip. Keep going till the first frosts.

Cut back fading lavender, to the base of flowering stems.

odd human voice over the fence. Children playing. I get frustrated if it's raining and I have to pace indoors with imminent cabin fever. It's wonderful to look out on something beautiful, and walk through a bit of garden to the front door. It calms me. It reduces my blood pressure. Even looking at something green does that.

What do you think? Why do you garden? Or do you? How can I help you feel that first *frisson* of falling in love, which can lead to a lifelong love affair? "I do miss my garden", some of the 80 and 90 year old Braemar Lodge residents say.

Just getting one often seems to be the catalyst. That's what Hugo told me, and I think my first minuscule plot in London did it for me. I was drunk with power and possibilities. I looked at it

with a wild surmise, silent upon a peak in Darien. Steph started work when her last child was born, "and I had the time." Poor old time, it does get blamed for a lot. So does the weather. It's always too this or too that. Hark, I hear the birds of rationalisation flapping overhead. Hey, once you fall, you find the time and you don't give a shit about the weather. There's always something to do and it makes you feel so good to have achieved it.

"Gardening encompasses everything that is right in my life", says Sara. "It's the whole ethos of living deep within me for little seeds to have the wonderful results that I myself can produce. There's a huge sense of accomplishment."

So don't let anything hold you back. The point of writing this book was to take away the mystique

Frog – or is it a toad? – in lavender cuttings.

JOBS THIS MONTH

- Spur prune gooseberry sideshoots and currants, red and black. Cut this year's fruited raspberry and loganberry canes off at base, and tie in new green ones.

- Prune wisteria. Spur prune new whippy side shoots down to 6 - 8", to encourage flowering, and new main branch growth to where you want it to go, and tie in.

- Cut back fading lavender, down to the bottom of the flower stems. Scissors or shears. Take some cuttings from non-flowered stems. (See **July**.)

- Take other cuttings, eg rosemary, sage and penstemons.

- Cut back plants overflowing onto the lawn, and reseed where grass has died.

- Keep digging up potatoes – main crop should be ready about now.

- Start scarifying the lawn. Keep mowing too. It'll probably look a fright in August.

- Buy bulbs, biggest, firmest. Start planting daffs and crocuses, tulips November.

- Prune buddleia. Dead head generously, chopping off the top third of the branches.

- Fill gaps with late-flowering perennials, eg heleniums or rudbeckia.

- Keep feeding camellias every couple of weeks. (Rain)water them, if it's dry.

and fear. Are you still mystified and fearful? **It's only gardening** – blazon it in fireworks in the night sky. Go out and make mistakes. I fervently believe you just need to start. Anywhere. Ten Simple Rules in January is a good place. Think which flowers you love, then look them up – one of the Hessayon paperbacks will tell you which conditions they like, and the labels on new plants will too. Gradually build up a list, and while you're thinking, keep the garden tidy and stuff in something colourful, like marigolds, to cheer you. If it doesn't work, tear it out and start again. Who gives a toss?

Try these too: take on one thing you feel confident about, eg mowing the lawn, and not only will it make the whole garden look better, but it's one less thing to pay a gardener to do. They cost £15 an hour around here. Trim the lawn edges. Do an exciting job after a mundane one. And reward yourself: a bottle of *rosé* in the fridge, a mug of hot chocolate, or in my case an ice lolly. Nothing like a good suck. It really doesn't matter where you start, or when you start, or what trick you use, as long as you start. The longer you leave it the worse it will get. Weeds grow, grass grows, creepers climb and climbers creep. Pull up the sycamore seedlings while the kettle's boiling. And of course the more we learn about something, the more likely we are to become interested. Who was it said a journey starts with a single step? Start with one rose, one pot, one bed, one weed. Anything. **Just do it**: embroider on a cushion. Go for it, my friends. Let me not have slaved over this book in vain. Blimey, so much for 'a small moment'. Here endeth the lesson. Let's go get a drink.

SNAILS AND MIRANDA'S GARDEN
Congratulations to my cousin Miranda, who got married to Adam last month, and now is temporarily poised in a rented cottage called simply No.79 name of village, in Wiltshire. I am off to visit her and the new light of my life, her son Archie (and her tabbycat) next week. While she was living in Brighton, she sent me some pictures of her garden and asked me for any ideas on unappetising plants to snails and caterpillars. Oh dear, our universal problem. So this might be the place to mention you

The ménage à trois *pigeons at lunch.*

never see snails on lavender, curry plant (helichrysum), rosemary, sage, camellias, any shrub with thick leathery leaves, like eleagnus, bay, laurel, euonymus, clematis, grasses, paeonies, phlox and hardly ever on roses. What to do about them? Brace yourselves: not pellets. Just put the buggers into a lidded pot with salt in the bottom and shake 'em all about. It's instant. As to caterpillars, just pick them off and put them on the lawn for the robins.

SAGE TEETH TIP Rub your teeth with a few sage leaves – completely removes plaque and leaves them squeaky clean.

September

The red-breast whistles from a garden-croft;
And gathering swallows twitter in the skies.

John Keats, 1795 – 1821. To Autumn.

OK *Time to go time. September's here: the garden may be running out of steam, but now it's cooler weather we can spring to life again, there's work to be done. The great tidy up can begin, while we fill gaps with new plants. Some of the blackberries are over, but the pears, apples and crabapples are ripening, and the tortoiseshell spiders are weaving webs in the borders. Hello, hello, anybody out there?*

2011

2nd	Holly berries ripening on Charlotte's tree – a month early this year.	16th	Heron flies at 7.30 am, perched on treetop. Branch broken on 'Conference' pear it's so laden. Pear chutney.
6th	Dark and stormy day – pears cascading off tree onto the lawn.	20th	Kingfisher flashing along Avon by Crane Bridge.
7th	Drove to Miranda's through hay stacks and swiss rolls. Sedum is out.	24th	Dead heading marigolds and helenium, scattering seeds as I go.
8th	New clematis 'Kermesina' finally in flower, ditto *texensis* 'Gravetye Beauty.'	25th	Hummingbird hawkmoth hovering in *Verbena bonariensis.*
9th	8am mixed tits in apple trees: blue, coal, great and longtailed.	26th & 28th	Red kite circling high over Salisbury, cruising on the thermals.
12th	Honeysuckle flowering again.	28th	Indian summer: temps in 70s. Shorts on.

September, month of spiders' webs, one of Sam's close-ups, beware, arachnophobes, wonderful word.

Exquisite work of art above my log pile, sorry to put two in.

LAWN TIME AGAIN, OH GOODY. We are approaching the end of the mowing season, thank God, and the grass is greening up. Now is time for the Autumn treatment. You want a perfect lawn? Abandon hope all ye who enter here. You will not find the word perfect in my vocabulary, supremely not in relation to a garden. Lawns are a necessary evil: a patch of green cools the eye in the midst of colourful chaos, but they are tedious affairs – it's worth questioning whether you really need one. Too tiny or too shady, you may as well pave. Sometimes I need a man in my life. They seem to be born with the lawn gene, along with a taste for spotted dick.

However, we've got one, so brace yourself, Norman. Here is what a lawn needs:

1. **Feeding** in autumn – ideally before the end of this month. Can be bought in packages, granules or soluble. Kills moss too. Mow beforehand and if using granules do it just before rain expected, or you'll have to water in.

2. **Scarifying** September/October. Rake out all the dead grass (thatch) and moss, stuff a handful in an upturned pot for a bumble bee's nest and bury in the ground. Make leaf mould by raking up the leaves, preferably when wet, put in pierced plastic bag, tie at neck, and scatter around woodland plants after about six months.

3. **Tining** (spiking), to improve drainage, with special rolling pricker or garden fork. Shove it right down in rows across lawn about 6 inches apart. I do both these jobs over several days or weeks, in 20 to 30 minute sessions. Little and often as always.

4. **Mowing** again dammit, November/December.

5. **Ignoring**, despairing, January to March. Get mower serviced.

6. **Mowing** weekly from say March/April to August. (Cut grass can be used to mulch around fruit trees and drought-hating plants like phloxes and Japanese anemones.)

7. **Feeding** in May: top dressing 5 parts Ecomix to 1 BFB. Make up barrow full, shovel onto lawn, brush in. Hard work, do over several days/weeks.

8. **Sitting** on all summer. Don't worry if it goes brown and naked, first rains will replenish.

9. **Killing** weeds with lawn spot weedkiller – just walk up and down squirting. Banish cats and children from garden until dry.

If it is beyond help, you may need Nos 10 & 11:

10. **Turfing** a new lawn, between October and February. Get a professional who will chuck out all the stones and lay it perfectly flat, unlike mine, laid by me, a novice.

11. **Watering** and not walking on for the first few weeks of a new lawn.

Book to get: Dr DG Hessayon's *The Lawn Expert*. All the Hessayon paperbacks are excellent.

CRABAPPLE JELLY TIME. If you know someone who has a tree of 'John Downie' crabapples, take a bucket to collect some. This is usually an early September job, but this year they were ripe in August. Pick them off the tree, rotting windfalls are no good for making crabapple jelly – it'll grow penicillin. Here's what I do:

Chuck crabs into washing up bowl of water and sluice around to wash. Tip into preserving pan. Add water up to half the height of the crabs, stew on low heat with lid on for half an hour, forty minutes, stirring from time to time. When done, mash a little then spoon slush into jelly bag supported on legs over bowl. Leave to drip overnight. Resist urge to press down with spoon or it will go cloudy. Measure liquid and for every pint allow 3/4 lb of granulated sugar, warmed in a low oven. (They usually say 1 lb to 1 pt but I think this makes it too sweet.) When you take it out, shove some clean jamjars and their lids in. Tip sugar into warmed-up juice, to which you've added juice of 2 or 3 lemons, and a bag of lemon peel, and stir to dissolve, before boiling like buggery (technical term) till it reaches setting point. This comes pretty quickly, there being so much pectin in crabapples. Add knob of butter to reduce scum – there's still a lot of skimming, but it's worth it to get a clear jelly. Test on cold saucer in fridge, till it sort of skins over and moves in a jellylike way. Ladle into hot jars, cover with wax tops and put lids on. All fruit jellies – apple and mint, quince – are made like this, and are brilliant secret ingredients in stews and gravies, or with lamb, ham or mousetrap. For extra glamour, put a piece of lemon peel in each jar, but if you do that you'll need to let the jelly cool down for 10 or 15 minutes before ladling, or it will just float on the top.

BULB PLANTING Well, daffs, and crocuses. As last month, get as many daffsandcrocs as you can afford and bear to spend time planting. Biggest,

Crabapples 'John Downie', the best for making jelly.

Time to plant daffs: here are 'Jetfire' and 'Ice Follies' behind, two favourites.

firmest. Just a few make all the difference. Buy loose if possible. My favourite daffodils are 'Ice Follies' – palest yellow and white and utterly reliable. I also love the late flowering old 'Pheasant's Eye' – white with red eye – but so many others disappear, as did some of a 10kg cheap and cheerful bag of mixed daffs from Scats after the first year.

I quite like them coming up in grass too. The small ones, like Wordsworth's host of yellow ones, *Narcissus pseudonarcissus*. Not too many, unless you have a wild area, because you can't mow the lawn until six weeks after they've flowered – the leaves must die down naturally. Remove a piece of turf about a foot square, dig down a bit further (apply the rule of planting bulbs at least twice their total height), throw in a handful of bonemeal and another of grit, to help drainage, place bulbs about a couple of inches apart, fill in hole, replace turf, stamp down, and wait till the spring. Or scatter handfuls about and use a bulb planter to dig them in where they fall.

This year too I've planted the miniature white daffs 'Thalia' around the graves of Harpo and his brother Groucho. In November I'll add 'White Triumphator' lily-flowered tulips.

BUYING TULIP BULBS   Yes, August and September are the months to get those too, but not to plant them. You'll have the best choice if you buy them now – again, fattest and firmest. I know, it does take a bit of effort to think about this, when you are still mourning the end of summer, such as it wasn't, but if you wait till November you may only find the smallest and soggiest. If you can't find them loose, buy in nets, but poke them first. If any are soggy, don't get them. Lay them out unwrapped in a cool dry place. If you put them in too early they are prone to tulip fire disease. (See **November**.)

SEDUMS: THE GOOD AND BAD NEWS   Bad news is they're extremely boring plants that fall over a lot. Good is that they start flowering in September and beggars can't be choosers at this time of year. Also, bees like them. As already mentioned in May, it's worth trying the Chelsea Chop when they start sprouting, ie cut them back by half, and they come out short, stubby plants, a great improvement. The normal one is 'Autumn Joy.' An interesting botanic detail: I got the choppings to root in jamjars of water – all from a white plant, maybe 'Iceberg' – and when they came up, some were the dreary pink. Good way to increase plants though.

HOMAGE TO PIET AT BRAEMAR   Lesley, the gardener at Braemar Lodge, and I have been discussing sedums lately. We are trying to make more of one of the best and sunniest beds, planted with ever increasing shrubbbbbbbbs – OK for landscaping when the home was built, but so boring and green for residents to look at. Turns out we both admire Piet Oudolf, the Dutch designer who popularised "prairie planting" – inspired by the American prairies, amazingly. This means lots of grasses and large numbers of the same plants in huge drifts. So we have chopped down several viburnums and ouch-what-is-the-point-of-bloody-berberis, with thorns an inch long, one of which went straight through my glove and got stuck in my thumb. We are planning colour – sedums, yes, echinacea, penstemons, heleniums, grasses and 90 multicoloured 'Apeldoorn Elite' tulips. "Shall we call it the Homage to Piet border?" I asked her last week. Yeay.

> ## Thought of the month
> *"As long as one has a garden, one has a future, and if one has a future, one is alive."*
> Frances Hodgson Burnett, author of
> *The Secret Garden.*

Cosmos 'Purity' – a tremendous faff to grow from seed, but worth it to have a bed looking like this.

THE JOY (AND PAIN) OF COSMOS Taking Sarah Raven's (sigh) advice I decided to have a go at Cosmos last year, to take over from the *Allium cristophii* in the 'Apeldoorn' bed. It was a real palaver: you plant them indoors in Jiffy pellets, or two seeds into individual pots, and when they have three pairs of leaves, pinch out the centres. Harden them off gradually by taking them out for an airing in the daytime, and back indoors at night. This was a slow process. When they got to about 6 inches of weedy growth (and when all frosts are over, these are tender plants), I planted them out, watered them when I remembered, and there they languished until long after the *cristophii* had dried. The bed looked like shit, and I was despairing, but come September was full of beautiful white daisy-like flowers, 'Purity', with loads of buds, and all October too, till a sudden frost on the 27th zapped them. Sarah says they take ten weeks to get into flower. If you plant them earlier than I did, say in mid April, you can put them out at the beginning of June, and they could be in flower by er, July? Or alternatively, they might not. Colin the gardener says these Mexican flowers need equal amounts of

JOBS THIS MONTH

- Time for autumn lawn feed. Mow first, then sprinkle or water in. Kills moss too.

- Keep scarifying. Try and find someone with an electric scarifier. Then tine.

- Clear up, cut down, bonfire. Summer's over. Leave seedheads for goldfinches.

- Mulch clematisses with manure or compost, after forking in some bonemeal.

- Start feeding birds again. Wash out water bowls daily, to prevent green and chaffinches picking up some fatal parasite, say RSPB.

- Plant out wallflowers in permanent positions. Water in, pinch tops out after a week.

- Plant new plants or move things, while the ground is still warm.

- Plant daffodils, crocuses and any other bulbs except tulips.

- Cut back later lavender flowers, to bottom of flowered stems.

- Scatter hardy seeds, like poppies.

- Feed camellias every two weeks until the end of the month, then stop.

day and night in order to make buds, and therefore (do you follow me) don't get going till September. This year about six seeded among the rudbeckia I thought would fill the bed, but have been pathetic. Next year I'll do cosmos again, starting to collect seeds now, and planting earlier – they're worth it.

STOP PRESS POTATO NEWS Top spuds: Nadine, Yukon Gold and *Santé*. Try 'em.

Lavender again, intertwined with Clematis texensis *'Princess Diana', a happy alliance.*

The new Clematis viticella *'Kermesina' finally flowered, hooray.*

'Conference' pears: so laden this year, a branch broke.

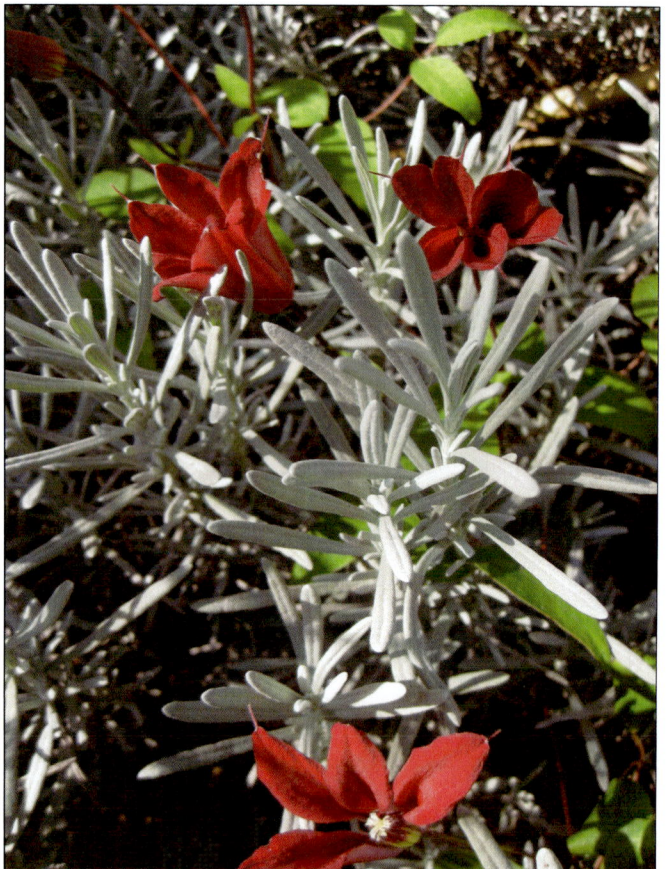

Same lavender, with new C. texensis 'Gravetye Beauty'.

October

Casually then… the Mole turned his talk to the harvest that was being gathered in, the towering wagons and their straining teams, the growing ricks, and the large moon rising over bare acres dotted with sheaves. He talked of the reddening apples around, of the browning nuts, of jams and preserves and the distilling of cordials; till by easy stages such as these he reached mid-winter, its hearty joys and its snug home life, and then he became simply lyrical.

Kenneth Grahame, 1859 – 1932. The Wind in the Willows.

First of October and the Virginia creeper is bright red on the shed, the sun's out and a proper wind, more than a breeze, is slamming doors and whipping my green spotty curtain dry on the line. Leaves are pouring off the trees and the plum is almost bare. It's the month of Michaelmas and Michaelmas daisies. When all else fails, leave it to the asters. Indian summer in 2011 continues, then it turns chilly for the first time.

2011

5th   Dawn chorus reduced to a tweet, around 7.

9th   Arbutus alive with huge striped bumbles, flowers out on sunny afternoon.

10th   Disaster: 'Madame Alfred Carrière' has blown down. Now we know why they say prune roses and check ties at this stormy time of year.

14th   Rudbeckia 'Irish Eyes' out at last. One from a whole packet. Hopeless.

17th   Blackbird's back. Where do they go all summer? Must get more mealworms.

20th   Frost on cars. Primroses.

23rd   Sparrowhawk lands on plum tree.

26th   Autumn colours – maples and beeches in shades of mahogany and satinwood.

27th   17 goldfinches on plum.

30th   Clocks go back.

CLINGERS, CREEPERS AND CLIMBERS When I bought this ugly pebbledashed house, which my brother christened The Hammer House of Horror, it was for many good reasons, one of which was the Boston ivy that covered the west wall and disguised the pebbledash a little. Supported by an ancient twisted trunk, *Parthenocissus tricuspidata* (get your teeth in) was patchy, due to past hacking, but I was delighted to find this self-clinger, with little pads on its feet, bright shiny green in the summer, and bright shiny copper in the autumn, buzzing with hoverflies as the seeds pop. In addition, Virginia creeper (*Parthenocissus quinquefolia*, I ask you) was flapping about on the corner. This is not so much a clinger as a creeper, and needs tying in or at least encouraging to climb. I dug it up and shoved it down by the shed, which it now completely covers. Equally striking in autumn, it's a bit more enthusiastic for growing on a north wall, as it does there. It's a terrific dangler, as the A said to the B. At The Red Lion pub, in town, it falls over the coaching arch like a long red fringe.

Climbers are a wonderfully economical way of covering a naked house, or a hideous outbuilding. Also they will provide privacy by racing up a piece of trellis. But choose carefully, according to the space available. A fast growing golden hop, with its startling lime green leaves, is a bit of a mixed blessing, as it grows so enthusiastically – up telegraph poles for example. So choose the site wisely, and give it enough room. It is damn difficult to get up on a long ladder and chop a hop down from the chimney. Or out of the gutters, which it blocks with irritating frequency.

Then of course there are climbing and rambling roses, and numerous clematae.

The choice is yours. Climbers soften up a house like mine, and even a beautiful one can look bleak without one. Good for birds too, and for a small

garden, giving maximum vertical effect without occupying too much floor space. Or try them climbing up an old fruit tree, as did Our Gertie.

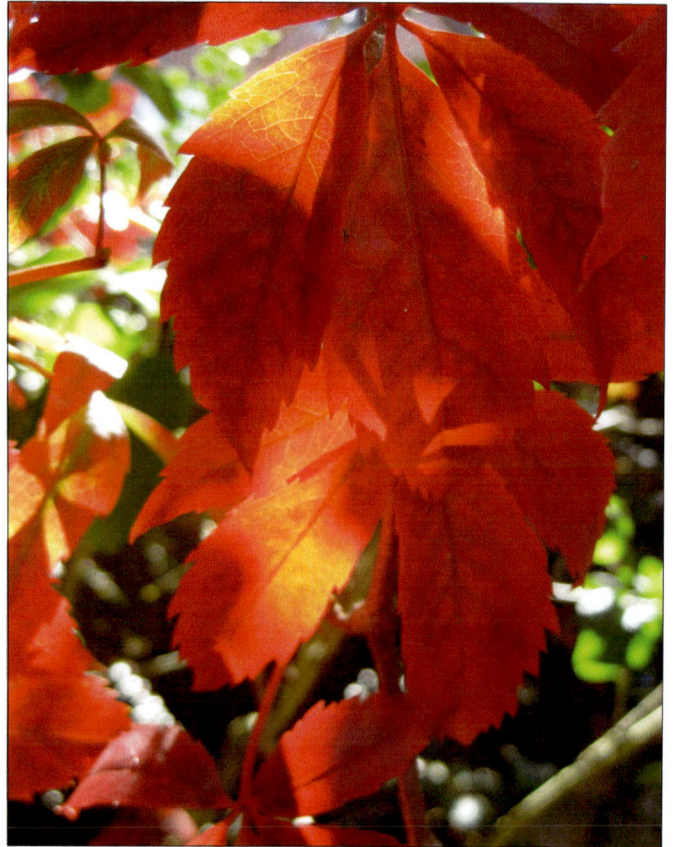

Virginia creeper, a ruby red clinger, happy to grow on a north wall.

Stipa arundinacea in spring, with yellow alyssum and 'Golden Apeldoorns'.

SCRAP SOME THINGS Now's the time, while out there on an Indian summer afternoon, leaning thoughtfully on your spade, accompanied by a robin, to cast a critical eye over the garden. Annual review. What's been good? What's got too big? What are you bored with? What's died? Notes in a gardening diary throughout the year can be helpful. It's time to be brave and maybe brutal. Jettison something, prune something, resite something. When in doubt, dig it out. As long as you give it a good drink before and after you'll probably get away with it. As the trees shed their leaves you can see their shapes better, and decide if any need lopping or even felling. Beware Tree Protection Orders if in a Conservation Area – talk to the Tree Officer in the Planning office. Winter is a good time to trim lilacs or fruit trees, while they are dormant in December or January. If you gain a space, either through death or destruction, you gain an opportunity to plant something you really like. I have just got rid of a ceanothus tree, and now have space for five *Rosa rugosas*, very exciting.

GREAT GRASSES A recent convert to grasses, I now couldn't do without them, particularly in September and October, when so much else has been and gone, and they come into their own, gracefully waving about in the breeze. God bless Piet Oudolf. I saw two Piet borders at RHS Wisley, fields of colour, interspersed with waving grasses, leading down to the new hothouses, at their best about now. I am far too basic to understand why I need to learn about forty different leaf shapes from the Royal Horticultural Society, and was surprised to be unimpressed by Wisley, sorry, but Piet's prairies alone were worth the entry fee.

I have garden designer and writer Daniel Pearson to thank for recommending *Stipa arundinacea*, now called *Anemanthele lessoniana*, good luck with that – an evergreenish reddish grass, to soften up the herbaceous border. And it does. Just over knee high, it fills gaps elegantly, and reproduces prolifically from red clouds of feathery flowers. I have them all over the place, including gravel paths, a favourite breeding ground for self-seeders. My second favourite is *Stipa gigantea* (I can never resist anything called gigantea.) Plant them where the setting sun can shine through the 6ft high oaty flower heads. I have seven on the Med bed, making wide fountains at ground level. All this one requires is to cut down its spikes in the autumn, and tug out all the dead grass underneath. I think I have a hedgehog nesting under one. Round the corner is *Stipa tenuissima*, blond hair blowing in the wind. When all *Stipas* and evergreen grasses are actively growing, from April to August, you can cut them back by a third to a tufty shape. You will often find youngsters hiding under their skirts. Deciduous ones can be cut to the ground, late February to late March.

Great grasses: Stipa gigantea, six foot high and beautiful against the sun.

JOBS THIS MONTH

- Tickle up and top dress, with compost, leaf mould, lawnmowings, bonemeal or BFB. Part of autumn tidying, empty beds or full.

- Mulch clematisses with compost or manure, after forking in some bonemeal.

- Keep scarifying lawn Yes, I know it's a pain. Get out the rake and just do a patch every day. Time for tining too (see **September**).

- Keep planting out wallflowers.

- Dig dig dig dig dig.

- Still time to plant new plants, and divide old ones, while ground is still warm.

- And still time to take cuttings of half hardy perennials, ie penstemons, hebe, salvias. Overwinter indoors.

- Dig out rest of spuds before slugs get 'em. Now all is safely gathered in.

IN PRAISE OF MICHAELMAE What a relief to have something come out in October, in a determined fashion, when all the plants about them are losing the will to live, and demanding to be cut down and put to bed for a few months. Hibernate, yes, exactly, as do we. I have noticed achillea, antirrhinums and dahlias from the bus. But the October stars are definitely Michaelmas daisies. Our friend *Aster frikartii* 'Mönch' is still flowering away in his nine massive mounds of mauve, though somewhat battered by the October gales. Three months he's been going. The babies are doing better than the parent. Every couple of years I split one up, in March. Aster 'Vasterival' is coming out now – loads of tiny lilac flowers. Aster 'Alma Pötschke' – bright pink – is reluctantly getting the message; she's not as strong as the others. Splitting her two years ago, the babies entirely disappeared. Michaelmas daisies used to be mildew-ridden things, but new and improved *novae angliae* (New England asters) and *novi belgii* (New York asters – eh?) are mildewless. Shit, I'm beginning to sound like an RHS plant geek, pardon.

And talking of plant geeks … the peerless whom God preserve Sarah Raven in her *Telegraph* "trialling" (dreadful word) said her top Michaelmae were *Aster novae-angliae* 'Primrose Upward' – a bright, strong pink, 'Andenken an Alma Pötschke' (mine), 'Violetta' and 'Cliff Lewis' – rich purple; *Aster novi-belgii* 'Carnival' – a brilliant deep pink. Take 'em or leave 'em – Alma is the only one I've tried. Worth seeking out a few, including of course Mr *A.f.* 'Mönch", which Sarah inexplicably forgot, but you knew I wouldn't. Cut them down after they've flowered, and look forward to next October. 'They all split easily, in March. With 'Mönch', I divided one of my original three clumps into five plants. All flowered brilliantly in the same year.

In praise of Michaelmae: let us all bow down and worship Aster frikartii 'Mönch' and Clematis tangutica.

The Arbutus tree flowers and fruits at the same time, attracting butterflies like this Red Admiral.

Aster 'Vasterival' – another Michaelmas that likes being split up.

And one that doesn't: 'Andenken an Alma Pötschke', what a mouthful. Lovely, though.

Morning glory 'Heavenly Blue'

Marigolds, cheerful, faithful.

November

No shade, no shine, no butterflies, no bees,
No fruits, no flowers, no leaves, no birds – November!

Thomas Hood, 1799 – 1845. 'No!

*T*he month of foggy, frosty mornings, and sunny days. The mistle thrushes return to the mistle tree and the plum, with their chubby bodies and freckly chests, and with luck we may see a few redwings pause in their journey south. The month that mad dogs and Englishmen go for muddy post Sunday lunch walks among the skeleton trees in the November gloom. Anyone seen my wellies?*

2010

2nd   Avenue of golden beeches en route Romsey. Also *Rhus typhina*.

8th   Pigeons have devoured the holly berries on top third of Charlotte's tree.

11th   Armistice Day. Wild and windy. Eiderdown back on bed.

12th   Finished planting tulips, 90 'Apeldoorn Elites' in Gaudy bed. Can't wait. Titillation in the plum tree: Blue, Great, Long-tailed and Coal.

14th   Mistle Thrush is back (on 13th last year.)

15th   V formation of geese flying south against the rising half moon.

16th   Fr-r-r-osty and foggy, yesterday and today, frosted cobwebs.

24th   Flash of black, white and red: Great Spotted Woodpecker on plum tree.

27th   Snow. 'Venosa Violacea' clematis still in bud.

29th   Mahonia out, yellow sprays next to red berried Cotoneaster.

THE LAST ROSE OF SUMMER Yeah, there are still some pathetic rain-drenched blooms desperately trying to flower at the tail end of a long spindly branch. As ever they are reaching for the sun, and reaching in vain in November. I hack the whole lot back, so they won't be damaged by winter gales. It feels kinder to put them out of their misery. When to prune roses? Whenever the hell you like. (Well, OK, not in frost or snow.) You can't hurt a rose by pruning it. The more you do, the happier it will be. I can hardly bear to see the etiolated unloved specimens in the gardens I pass on my way to the town, and itch to attack them with my red loppers. Let your mantra be: **When in doubt, prune.** (See **March**.) Prick it out in busy lizzies on a roundabout.

Tulip planting month: 'Apeldoorns' interplanted with yellow wallflowers…

PLANTING BARE ROOT ROSES Cheaper this way, they arrive in November. Keep well wrapped until you are ready to plunge them into a bucket of water while you dig a decent hole the shape of their roots, which may be spread out in a circular shape or even to one side. Make up a mixture of John Innes No. 3 compost, some peat-free ditto, garden soil, bonemeal, and for good luck some Mycrooccial fungi thingy (*Rootgrow, and it's*

mycorrhizal. Ed.) I also add composted manure. Place rose so its grafting lump will be about an inch below the soil. Fill in hole with this mixture, firm in at halfway stage, shaking the rose a little so that compost settles down between its roots, and carry on till it's filled in. Stamp in lightly, attach the label, and water well. Roses usually come already pruned; if not, prune back to outward facing bud, yes I know you know that. If there is likely to be a delay of more than ten days before you can plant a bare root rose, or any other bare root plant, heel it in to a trench or hole somewhere in the garden, and make sure it's watered. It's important the roots don't dry out.

PLANTING TULIPS At last I can take my baskets of bulbs out of the sitting room, where I've kept them since September, and start the highly enjoyable job of guaranteeing a fantastic display next spring. Where would we be without the glorious early 'Orange Emperor', the reliable red and yellow 'Apeldoorn' family, the exquisite lily-flowered 'Ballerina', 'Red Shine', 'China Pink', and the hideously named but pure 'White Triumphator'? Not to mention the real show-offs, the parrots. Crouching on a foam kneeler in the

…and here with forget-me-nots. What do you think?

November winds, sharp trowel in hand, I give each hole a sprinkling of bonemeal, and a fistful of grit to help them survive the winter soggery. They say 9 inches deep prevents tulip bulbs being dug up by mice or squirrels, and encourages them to keep appearing. I'm not convinced: some do, some get fewer, some disappear, and some, like the 'Apeldoorns' (Darwin Hybrids), increase in number. You can also plant alliums at the same time, which will succeed the tulips. If you plant in groups, of say ten or twelve, plant a couple of inches apart.

COMPANION PLANTING Interplanting tulips, however, plant them singly 6 inches apart. Try forget-me-nots (just sprinkle them when you pull them up), wallflowers, pansies, single colour polyanthuses, or a C Lloyd suggestion, lupins, in between them. Be brazen: colour combinations can be stunning. The more exotic specimens, like parrots and lily-flowered, look good in terracotta Long Toms, £4.50 from B & Q, with John Innes No. 3 compost, on a bed of grit, with a handful of bonemeal below, and chipped slate above. They can be planted deeper in these tall pots, and you can fit about ten in, squashed together. They make a fine display in the first year, then probably diminish or die thereafter, so treat them more or less like annuals, and shrug your shoulders if they have to go. My best tulips come from **P de Jager & Sons Ltd**. Church Farm, Ulcombe, Maidstone, Kent ME17 1DN. Telephone 01622 840229, www.dejager.co.uk

THE BIG HACK BACK An exciting job in October and November is to get out on a sunny afternoon, boots on, barrow or big bags and secateurs akimbo, to start to tidy up the shambles. I leave seed heads till last, for the blue tits and goldfinches, but the rest is at my mercy. Nearly all perennials can be hacked to the ground, except the early flowerers you've probably already done, like philadelphus

and ceanothus, and the late bloomers like ceratostigma, hydrangea and penstemon, whose faded flowers and growth protect the plant from the winter cold. Safer to do these in March or April.

FEED THE BIRDS Tuppence a bag. Welcome sunflower hearts, in those plastic tubes, hung from or near a tree they can pop in and out of – they seem to like that. Grapes on the ground are swooped on by the blackbirds, though they are in dangerous territory, with Harpo around. Sunflower hearts are also enjoyed by the tits, green and chaffinches. There is a perpetual squabbling when fifteen goldfinches attempt to eat from six portholes. The clever ones have realised most of it gets dropped on the earth below. Don't forget bird water, much enjoyed too by the hedgehog.

A GOOD START With planting, as with children, you can't beat giving them a good start.

Thus speaks the wise old spinster of Salisbury. Yup. And that means preparation. I have said before, to the point where you will be screaming obscenities at me, how crucial preparation is. Boring, but crucial. Tempting as it is, don't get seduced by a load of sexy numbers and stuff them in any old how. Plants are only human: they need the right soil, food and drink in order to put down strong roots, so they can grow up into successful adults for many years. In this important planting month, take the trouble to give the new residents of your garden all that they require, and if you're not careful someone will accuse you of having green fingers. The God says it's a good time to establish some spring flowers in their new permanent homes. This gives them time to settle in over the winter. He suggests lupins, oriental poppies, carnations, anchusas, those bright yellow daisies doronicums, aconites, and aquilegias.

Season of mists… and colours of mahogany and satinwood.

Alliums can be planted at the same time as tulips,
here 'Purple Sensation', which will self seed.

THE FIRST FROSTS Beware the first frosts. I used to think it was the survival of the fittest in this garden. But this year, sod it, I'm going to bubble wrap my camellia pots, and fleece the plants overnight (take off during the day) if The Big Freeze is expected (see **March**.) I'm also putting two pots of red trailing geraniae in the shed. May survive. Take cuttings too if you can bear hideous Passchendaele stumps all winter.

AUTUMN AT GIVERNY I have mentioned Monet and his garden at Giverny, near Vernon, on the Seine, several times in this book, and these foggy mornings have reminded me that I went there for the first time in autumn. It was October, the end of the season, and there were very few people in the garden. Every now and again we would meet parties of schoolchildren, chattering like starlings, but mostly it was quiet, with Michaelmases and dahlias still just flowering, dew on the grass, and a few yellow leaves remaining on the apple trees.

Have you been there? The top half of the garden, the *Clos Normand*, a former orchard, stretches across a gentle slope outside the low pink house with green verandah and shutters. Only 1 hectare, it is laid out in a grid of long narrow 'paintbox' beds, either side of a wide path, *La Grande Alleé*, leading down from the house to the road that runs along the bottom. Over the path are iron arches of climbing roses, and below orange and yellow nasturtiums, *les capucines*, stretch out their arms to meet in the middle, as they are now doing across my front path. Through a slightly gruesome tunnel under the road you make your way to the Japanese water garden – a separate area, bought by Monet in 1893, and made by him diverting the *Ru*, a tributary of the *Epte*, after a prolonged fight to get permission. No water lilies of course in October, just the leaves floating on the surface, the red liquidambars reflected in the water, the willows weeping, and the Japanese bridge draped with fading wisteria.

Monet died in 1926, having lived in the house for 43 years, bringing up his large family, and as we all know painting the garden in its every season. It was his obsession and his main inspiration. So many photographs show the bearded old boy at his easel, smoking a *Caporal*, and wearing a smock and a battered straw hat. Monet is still there. I have never visited another garden where the spirit of the man who made it is stronger. No matter how many schoolchildren, how many sketching students, how many clicking cameras, no matter what time of year, or time of day, Claude Monet is still going out to paint the water lilies, followed by his daughter carrying his canvases, and pausing in a clearing by the pond to check his 'Crimson Ramblers' for greenfly. Inside the colourful interior of the house you can almost hear the crusty old martinet, barking orders at his family or bellowing the Toreador's song from *Carmen* if his painting was going well. Do go to Giverny if you've never been, or even if you have. It's one place to visit before you die.

Giverny opening (2011) Daily 9.30 am to 6 pm, from 1st April to 1st November. Entry 8€, disabled, 4€; children and students 5€; children under 7, free. Address: Fondation Claude Monet, Rue Claude Monet, 27620 Giverny, France. www.giverny.org/gardens/fcm/visitgb.htm

PS. Forgive me for the following: Trevor, the blindmaker, walked through the garden the other morning to put up my new blue check kitchen blinds, paused and said: *"This garden is like something out of a Monet painting."* The impossible dream.

JOBS THIS MONTH

- Plant tulips and alliums.
- Plant bare root roses, shrubs, climbers and trees.
- Split day lilies (hemerocallis) If they get too congested they won't flower.
- Wrap up anything not frost hardy. Or don't.
- Dig over veg beds, forking in a few bags of manure (except spuds and onions.)
- Make paths, terraces and any other hard landscaping. If frost expected, protect new mortar with hessian sacks.
- Prune roses.
- Top up bird feeders and refill water daily.
- Take cuttings of half hardy perennials, ie penstemons, hebe, salvias. Overwinter indoors.

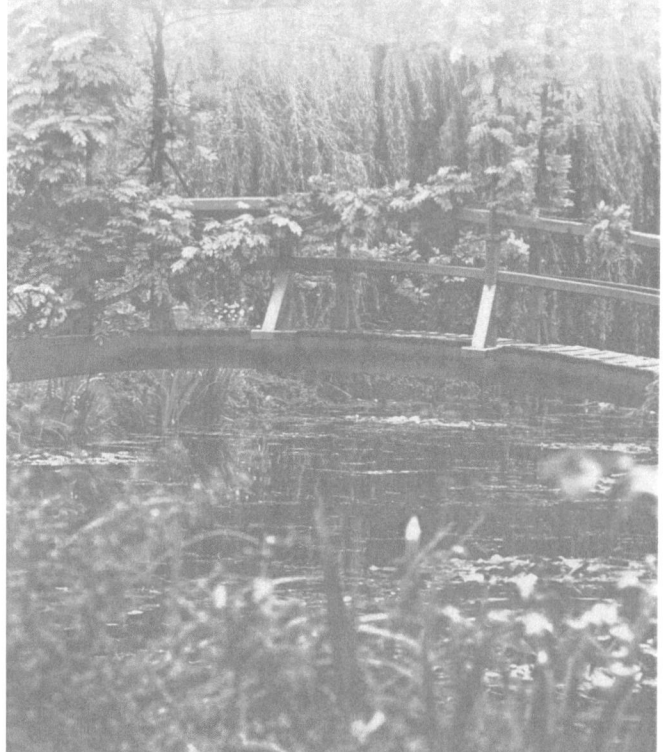

December

Ah, yet, e'er I descend to th' grave
May I a small house, and large garden have!
And a few friends, and many books, both true,
Both wise, and both delightful too!

Abraham Cowley, 1618 – 1667. The Mistress, or Love Verses.

Naked trees, save for clumps of mistletoe, and the sprays of 'Wedding Day' orange hips, mossy lawn covered with a thin layer of icing sugar, are what I see from my window as I write. The beautiful but lethal 'Mermaid' is still waving its arms in the wind, trying to flower. Let's rejoice that we may have returned to proper winter weather, and if plants die, we can plan their replacements while we sit round the fire. Crumpet, anyone?

The garden, on 2nd December.

2010

2nd Snow overnight. Winter Wonderland. Mistle thrush teetering on rose bough before flying across the road to Charlotte's laden hollies.

3rd Chaffinches, thrush, blackbirds, and a brambling around the feeding area, great spotted woodpecker on the plum. Proper snow last night, weighing down camellias.

7th Freeeeezing. Goldfinches eating rosehips, lilac, perovskia and echinops seeds, tits swaying on the *Stipas*.

11th Snow gone. Red streaks across the dawn sky. Shepherd's warning.

17th Redwing returns, stripe over eye, red armpits, speckly chest.

18th Snow again, blizzard till 10 am. About four inches.

22nd Flock of redwings now, about 15, stripping the hollies bare, and crapping all over my virgin snow.

25th Berries gone, most redwings gone. Such handsome birds. Bon voyage, guys.

26th Hoar frost. Minus 12 last night. No water 5 am. Wonderful Wessex Water came at 7 am and thawed out my mains pipe with a hairdryer. Still a gang of goldfinches and tits, thank God.

27th Blackcap in apple tree – or rather brown cap – Mrs.

Tête à tête daffodils, cheer yourself by buying a pot in the market and plant out later.

TÊTE À TÊTES Brrrrr. What a hellish month. Cheer yourself by buying a pot of three *T à T* daffs for £1.50 at Haskells in the market – the perfect post Christmas lunch present, and stand on a coolish window sill, or the cistern. When they're over, I tear them apart and stuff 'em in the ground and they come back year after year.

THINKING ABOUT PEARS Good time to cogitate on fruit trees. I have 'Conference' and 'Beth' here, to mate with each other, having got fatal scab (spray fungicide – one safe to use on fruit) on 'William's Bon Chrétien', that ugly fat but utterly mouthwatering ancient pear that was espaliered in a candelabra up the wall of Kate's house in the Close. In her new orchard the trees were pruned to just above head height by the faithful Mr Smith, including her 'John Downie' crabapples, which I was invited to pick and make into rose pink jelly. The great thing was you could reach them all. (See **September**.)

Choosing pears, find two which blossom at the same time, to cross fertilise, and thin pears to two fruits per cluster, 4" to 6" apart. 'Doyenne du Comice' is another delicious one worth trying. **Landford Trees** have a good choice. See **May** for details.

MAHONIA   I love mahonia, another yellow cheerer with a delicious lily of the valley scent (*Mahonia japonica* has the best.) Stick your nose into one as you pass somebody's garden, but be careful, it's prickly. Mine grows under the old apple tree, in semi shade. I keep it in check by hacking off the top every couple of years after flowering, and it then bushes up with more flowers.

CAMELLIAS   Now is the time for all good men to come to the aid of the camellia. That revolting black muck is sooty mould, the product of the scale insect making its home under the leaves and dripping its yuck onto the ones below. You can wash it off easily, though it's fiddly, with washing-up water and one of those little scourer sponges. It's very satisfying to reveal the shiny green again, albeit at the expense of a few buds, with which the bush is with any luck laden at this time of year. To prevent sooty mould, make a note to spray the camellia in June or July with Bio Provado Ultimate Bug Killer, when the eggs are laid, and do it now as well. Try and get it under its leaves; it's not easy, but Provado is systemic and will penetrate the whole plant. Don't breathe in the spray. Hold your breath. (More on camellias in **March**.) This will kill most of the eggs, and you may just have a few black leaves left, which you can wash.

Snow overnight on 2nd. Birdsteps.

Snow again on 18th: topiarised pots of boxes on the deck.

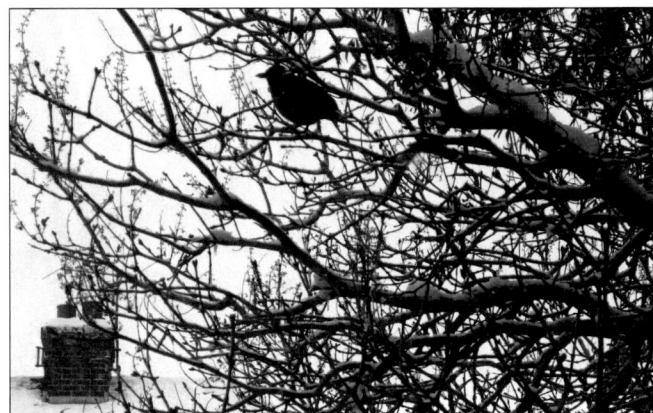

The singer of the sweetest song.
Here he is in the lilac, on the 20th at midday.

THE SHORTEST DAY While December may seem bleak midwinter, and the Christmas shtuck something to celebrate or tolerate, on December 21st those in the know are out planting their onions, which they will harvest, traditionally, on the longest, June 21st. After this shortest day, we peer into the morning darkness hoping for dawn to break a few minutes earlier, and for dusk to come a few minutes later. For hope springs eternal in the gardener's breast.

SOME SHADY CHARACTERS Walking round the garden, sniffing the mahonia, I made a list of things that are happy in the shade – more than you might think:

Ajuga (deep shade), **Alchemilla mollis** (anywhere), *Anemone nemorosa*, wood anemone (deep or dapply), **Bluebells** (dapply), **Buddleia** (some sun), **Chaenomeles** (ditto), *Clematis cirrhosa var* 'Balearica' (OK north wall), *Clematis* 'Perle d'Azur' (ditto), **Cotinus** (dapply), *Cotoneaster horizontalis* (anywhere), *Cyclamen hederifolium* (deep), *Erythronium dens canis* (dapply, not too dry), **Euonymus** 'Emerald 'n' Gold' (deep), *Euphorbia amygdaloides* (ditto), **Ferns** (deep, but not dry), **Foxgloves** (anywhere), *Fritillaria imperialis* (shade, rich soil, leafmould), **Hellebore** (deep or dapply), **Hostas** (ditto), *Iris foetidissima* (even dry shade), **Japanese anemones** (deep or dapply), **Lily of the valley** (ditto), **Mahonia** (ditto), **Primroses** (ditto), **Pulmonaria** (ditto), *Rose 'Canary Bird'* (OK on north wall), **Sarcococca, Christmas box** (shady), *Scilla siberica* and *bifolia*, self seeding blues (shady), **Snowdrops** (deep or dapply), **Tree paeony** (ditto), *Viburnum plicatum* 'Mariesii' (happly dapply), **Violets** (deep or dapply), **Virginia creeper** (anywhere, try and stop it.)

Most of these will appreciate some sunshine at least part of the day, or part of the year, and all could do with some rain from time to time. Dry shade under a permanent canopy, ie an effing conifer, is the most

Frosted fennel, early morning Boxing Day.

Shady characters: Hostas after rain, beautiful,
I grow in pots to deter invaders.

Another lime green shady character, after a shower.

difficult to populate. A good mulch of bark, compost or leafmould – made from last autumn's raked-up leaves and stored in pierced compost bags – helps to preserve what moisture there is.

FERNS I have started to grow these in the deep dapples under the mutilated old apple in the corner: these are the easiest, the strappy-leaved maidenhair, aka, get this, *Adiantum aleuticum*. It does OK now, thanks to recent filthy summers, though it can be a near thing in a hot spell, when you might have to revive it with a bucket of bathwater. I tried other ferns, but they were planted too close to the apple, and died. My neglect didn't help. I thought they'd get on with it. Which just proves what a crappy gardener I am. Live and let die.

A NEW DESIGN? If you are gazing dispiritedly out of the window at the falling snow or the frozen lawn, and after twelve months of toiling, the garden is still unsatisfactory (join the club), why not spend the winter thinking about redesigning it? It's a room you're going to see and be in every

Euonymus 'Emerald 'n' Gold' will grow anywhere,
and brighten up a dark wall.

day of your life, even if you're just carrying the washing out. Think of it as an extension to the house, and like an extension it will cost money. Hard landscaping is expensive, but skimping doesn't work. A grass path, for instance, may look good initially, but can soon get muddy and weed infested. Brick or stone paths, walls, terraces, enclosing flowerbeds, in a good strong shape, will be softened when the garden's planted, give it personality, and help you to come as near as dammit to being happy with it. Knight Frank say a good garden can add 13% to your house's value, and certainly makes it easier to sell than with a jungloid shitheap at the back. (Or the front: My God there are some round here. Rampant sycamore saplings, dandelions and those bloody wheely bins.) So I think it's worth saving for; it will be money well spent, and will cost less than a conservatory. For inspiration, there are loads of books on garden design in the library, and here are a few random thoughts:

- Good strong shape. Be brave.

- Break it up with trellises, beds, fences – all make it look bigger, surprisingly.

- Take design right across the garden to make it look wider.

- Hard landscaping materials should match or complement the house.

- Gravel reflects the light. 20mm minimum or cats use it for a loo.

- Paths should end in focal points – pot, statue – and be wide enough for 2 people.

- Favourite things – plants which make you smile. Make a list.

- Size isn't everything. You can transform the smallest space.

- K.I.S.S. – Keep it simple, stupid. **Less is more.** Embroider on a pillow.

If you decide to redo, make a plan, or contact a garden designer. They can turn a rough sketch into a scale plan, on which you can get quotes from 2 or 3 landscape companies. The first time I redid a garden was here in Salisbury. It didn't cost a fortune and opened my eyes to the possibilities of changing the exterior, in the same way you change an interior. You don't put up with somebody else's wallpaper – you decorate it in your style, or turn a place into what you want by knocking down a wall or blocking up a door. Go for it. And good luck.

JOBS THIS MONTH

- Start spraying Winter Wash on fruit tree trunks, and carry on till March. Prevents winter moths laying eggs, therefore caterpillars.

- Make sure your tetanus injection is up to date. All sorts of horrors can lurk in the soil, including shards of glass. Wear gloves, if you can bear it.

- Check stakes and ties. Some of the old ties may now be too tight and strangling the trunks or branches.

- Prune lilacs and fruit trees while dormant.

- Wash sooty mould off camellia leaves, and spray Bio Provado Ultimate Bug Killer.

- Dig dig dig dig dig. But not if muddy.

- Plant onions – on 21st.

Appendix

My Top 73 Must-Have Plants:

Winter

Buxus sempervirens 'Suffruticosa' What a mouthful. Normal box, clip into topiary for frosty winter skeletons, and solid shapes in summer shagginess.

Camellia x williamsii or j*aponica* Acid-loving, slow-growing bushes, vivid flowers.

Chaenomeles – japonica Prickly guys to be trained up wall or hang loose.

Daphne odora 'Aureomarginata' Tiny pink scented flowers on a small shrub.

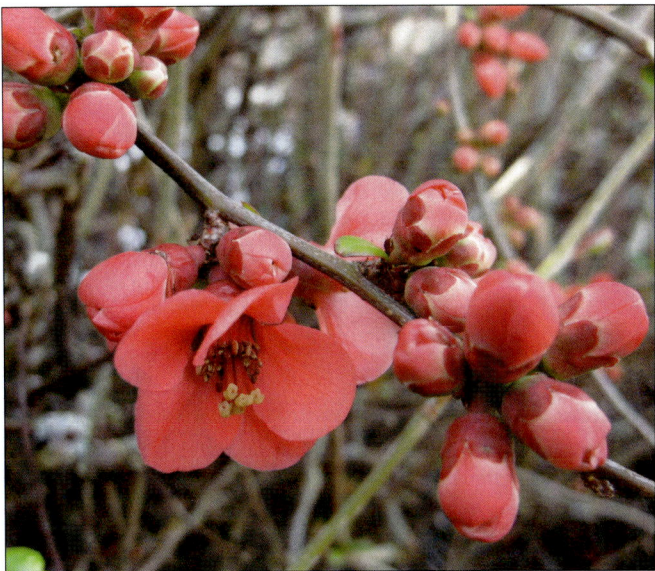

Another Chaenomeles, don't know which, in a neighbour's garden.

Eranthis hyemalis – **Winter aconite** Buttercup yellow surprise early in new year.

Euonymus Useful if dull variegated evergreen shrub, to light up a really rubbish spot.

Galanthus elwesii – **snowdrop** Taller than common, about 6", flowers slightly later.

Galanthus nivalis – **common snowdrop** Brightest and best in dim months Jan and Feb.

Helleborus orientalis – *hellebore*. Reliable, in every shade of mauve and maroon.

Helleborus niger Early flowering shade-loving white Christmas rose, self seeds.

Mahonia japonica Scented yellow-flowered prickly beast to scare off burglars.

Narcissus 'Tête à Tête' Utterly reliable little daffs, flowering in Jan and Feb.

Pulmonaria officinalis Blue and pink, spotty leaves, loved by bees, out early.

Spring

Alyssum, yellow Cascading over a sunny wall, often with its neighbour aubrietia.

Aubrietia massive mat of mauve falling over walls. Haircut after flowering.

Bluebell (*Hyacinthoides non-scripta***)** The common bluebell. Self seeds.

Aubrietia will grow anywhere, even by an Endless St downpipe.

Clematis montana, *pink or white. Flowers in April.*

Euphorbia characias '**Wulfenii**' Tall euphorbia, lime green flowers. Beware sap.

Forget-me-nots Pull up and shake about after flowering and you've got them for life.

Muscari or **grape hyacinth** Deep blue flower spikes from flabby green leaves, easy.

Narcissus '**Jetfire**' Tiny reliable yellow and orange daff. Just succeeds '*Tête à Tête*'.

Narcissus '**Ice Follies**' My favourite daff, yellow and white, flowers end of Feb.

Primula vulgaris – **primroses** Essential English woodland flowers. Self seed madly.

Rosa '**Canary Bird**' Early-flowering single yellow bush rose. Tough, treat rough.

Saxifrage Carpets pink or white, early March. Easy as pie. Haircut after flowering.

Tulips '**Apeldoorn**', '**Golden Apeldoorn**', '**Apeldoorn Elite**' Reliable Darwin Hybrids, upright guardsman red, plain no nonsense yellow, or red and yellow. March.

Viburnum plicatum '**Mariesii**' Elegant white-flowered tiered shrub, shady place.

Viola riviniana '**Purpurea**' Purple violet, purply leaves, seeds everywhere.

Wallflowers Glorious scent. Biennial, plant seed one year, flowers the next.

Summer

Allium hollandicum '**Purple Sensation**' and *cristophii* succeed tulips, 'P.S' early.

Buddleia or butterfly bush Essential July creature. 'Black Knight', deep purple.

Ceanothus '**Concha**' Ginormous dark blue bush. May not survive Arctic winters.

Centaurea cyanus, **cornflower** Blue. If you can grow them I may have to kill you.

Cephalaria gigantea, **yellow scabious** 6ft high statuesque plants. Bees go bananas.

Clematis viticella, any. Brilliant purple belters, stuff 'em in nice and deep, mulch 2" compost a foot around, on damp soil, and watch 'em go from about July. Prune Feb.

Clematis montana White or pink. Prolific climber and flowerer from April.

Digitalis, foxgloves Woodland native alive with buzzing and bees' bums. Self seeds.

Echinops or globe thistle Blue or white pricklies. Need support, loved by bees.

Fennel Tall elegant feathery plant, looks after itself. Useful for filling gaps.

Geranium, hardy Pink, white, purple, stick in anywhere and let it rip.

Honeysuckle You gotta have it. There's only one: 'Hall's Prolific.' Needs sun.

Iris sibirica 'Perry's Blue' was my original. Grow sunnyish place, split 3-yearly.

Knautia macedonica Worthy member of scabious family, maroony flowers.

Lavandula – **lavender** Stick to the old traditionals: *L. augustifolia* 'Hidcote', 'Twickel Purple', 'Munstead'. They're the toughest. *L. stoechas* borderline.

Lilium regale Waist-high, sweet-scented pinkish-white trumpets, *var. album* white. One stake. Plant sun, nr sitting area. Beware red lily beetle and pollen toxic to cats.

Nigella, love-in-a-mist Ubiquitous self-seeders in blue or white. But be grateful.

Papaver opium, **opium poppies** Scatter seeds and watch them reappear in the most unsuitable places. Red, pink, lilac, need no attention or support, and don't get eaten.

Perovskia '**Blue Spire**' Late summer, lavender blue, must have sun. Chelsea Chop.

Philadelphus '**Belle Etoile**' Classic white smelly flowering bush. Beware blackfly.

Paeonia, **paeonies** Exotic early summer beauties. Plant shallow in sunny spot. Also tree paeonies, more expensive, slower growing, taller, 'Argosy', pale yellow.

Rosa '**Bonica**' Pretty in pink, tireless small shrub rose. Chop to knee high in March

Rosa '**Compassion**' My top climber. Shiny dark green leaves, salmon flowers.

Rosa '**Gertrude Jekyll**' Shocking pink with addictive scent. Unofficial climber.

Rosa '**Leverkusen**' Lemon yellow scented climber, try with purple clematis.

Hardy geranium and bee: stick it in anywhere and let it rip.

Love-in-a-mist, Nigella, *and California poppies,* Eschscholzia. *Ubiquitous self-seeders.*

The 'Mermaid' rose, Monet's favourite: awkward but gorgeous.

Rosa 'Mermaid' Of all the awkward bastards that exist in the rose family, this must be the worst. I have never known a more ungrateful growing object. It attacks you with its vicious thorns each time you prune it, needs a lot of space and goes naked at the bottom. But when I see its giant lemon-coloured and lemon-scented single flowers at my bedroom window, I cannot help but smile at Monet's favourite rose.

Rosa 'Wedding Day' Rampant rambler, clusters of small white flowers.

Rosmarinus officinalis, rosemary Say no more, garden must-have. Leg of lamb.

Salvia officinalis, common sage Hairy green job, plant in sun. Smells good, looks good, pale mauve flowers. Scrub your teeth with a handful, removes plaque.

Stipa The favoured grass in the Currie household, *gigantea, arundinacea, tenuissima*.

Wisteria sinensis Romping lavender climber, or **W. floribunda 'Alba'**, white.

Autumn

Anemone x hybrida 'Honorine Jobert' Single White Japanese anemones.

Aster frikartii 'Mönch' Let us bow down and worship this essential perennial Michaelmas daisy, gazillions of violet daisies FOR OVER THREE MONTHS FROM JULY. Support and divide 3-yearly. See **March**. Named after *Jungfrau* peak.

Caryopteris x clandonensis 'Kew Blue' Mauvey-blue perennial with silvery leaves. Cut back in spring. Needs sun. So named because discovered in Clandon. How nice.

Ceratostigma willmottianum and plumbaginoides (blimey.) Bright blue small flowering shrub – prune in March – and its ground-hugging relative.

Cotoneaster horizontalis Tough old arching thing seeding in unpromising places.

Cyclamen hederifolium Suddenly appear, pink, red or white flowers. Self-seed.

Phlox paniculata Phlox rocks. No garden would be complete for me without them. fuchsia, coral, white or purple, they brighten a semi-shady place. Need support.

Verbena bonariensis Fashionable heliotrope, tallish see-through flowers. Prune in March to a foot from the ground. Good with grasses.

Trees

Bay Easy, evergreen, leaves for cooking, clip March, bush or tree, can be topiarised.

Laburnum Archetypal suburban tree, bright yellow explosions. Seeds poisonous.

Lilac Easy, old-fashioned tree or bush, scented purple, lilac or white flowers, single or double. If pruning needed, do in winter. "We'll gather lilacs"? Don't. Wilts.

Malus – apple, crabapple Essential. Blossom April, fruit September.

Pyrus – Pear Easy to grow, early white blossom. Most (except 'Conference') need cross pollination, check. Fruit September. Beware scab, spray fungicide (see page 72).

Plum 'River's Early Prolific.' Small tangy purple plums July and August, pre wasps.

'Wedding Day' rose cascading over old 'River's Early Prolific' plum tree.

And finally ….. How I agree with Mr Montaigne:

Je veux que la mort me trouve plantant mes choux
– I desire that death may find me planting my cabbages.

Michel Eyquem Montaigne, 1533 – 1592. Essais. To the Reader.

CJC.